The Truth About Buying
or Selling Your Home

Buyers Are Liars & Sellers Are Too!

Richard Courtney

A Fireside Book
Published by Simon & Schuster
New York   London   Toronto   Sydney

FIRESIDE
Rockefeller Center
1230 Avenue of the Americas
New York, NY 10020

FIRESIDE and colophon are registered trademarks
of Simon & Schuster, Inc.

For information regarding special discounts for bulk purchases,
please contact Simon & Schuster Special Sales at 1-800-456-6798
or business@simonandschuster.com.

Designed by William Ruoto

Manufactured in the United States of America

10 9 8 7 6 5 4 3 2 1

ISBN-13: 978-0-7432-8157-7
ISBN-10   0-7432-8157-8

To all the people who loved all the houses, but not enough to pay that much for them. ("Show us something else.")

And to all the people who wanted to sell their houses, but not enough to take that little for them. ("We're not going to give it away.")

And with extreme gratitude to all of those in between. ("We'll take it.")

Contents

Foreword

by Dave Ramsey
Three times *New York Times* bestselling author
and nationally syndicated radio host

I grew up in a real estate household. My dad started selling real estate when I was eight, and Mom sold houses back in the days when if you wore a pants suit instead of a dress you were considered unprofessional. Mom and Dad started their own company, built houses, and bought and sold a few that I, as a teenager, had the pleasure of painting and cutting down the four hundred-foot bushes to get them "sale ready."

So over twenty or so years ago, I entered the world of real estate. I have brokered, invested, rehabbed, managed sales teams, and of course dealt with buyers and sellers. It is with great pleasure that I introduce you to this fun and informative book *Buyers*

Are Liars & Sellers Are Too! They are. They don't mean to be. It is just that as a real estate agent, you encounter folks while they are messing at a very deep level with their psyches. When you move, you go crazy for a period of time. Real estate people see people at their worst, at the most-stressed-out times of their lives.

This wonderful book is a walk through the process of buying and selling. You will learn how to make one of the largest purchases you will ever make or sell one of your largest assets and do it right. I have never read a real estate book with as much humor and education packed between two covers. Old real estate dogs like me will laugh until they hurt, and clients will learn in a good-hearted way how the process of purchasing their slice of the great American dream can be done poorly or with style.

Preface

by Terry Watson
Nationally renowned real estate trainer and motivational speaker

For the average person, the stress associated with buying or selling a home can be compared to the stress associated with the death of a loved one, planning a wedding, or changing jobs. Let's face it: selling or buying your home is very emotional. In a fight in a dark alley, emotion will always beat logic. This is the reason doctors don't operate on family members.

I am a seasoned Realtor who speaks internationally and trains Realtors all over the United States, and I also conduct training for the National Association of Realtors. Recently, I sold my own condo, and although I consider myself a battle-scarred professional, the process was still very emotional, and, at times, even I was stressed out.

Awareness is sometimes curative. In *Buyers Are Liars & Sellers Are Too!* Richard Courtney, in a laugh-out-loud way, examines the complexity and emotional issues associated with the largest purchase of our lives, real estate.

It is my sad duty to report that in real estate there are two camps: the informed and the uninformed. This book will gain you admission into the camp of the informed. And it will help you deal with those who wandered into the other.

Given the prices of real estate these days, this book could be worth more than your car. The best compliment that I can give Richard is that I wish I had read this book before I bought my first house.

Introduction

Here is the story of *Buyers Are Liars & Sellers Are Too!* It seems there was this Realtor in Nashville, Tennessee, hereinafter referred to as "I." And I began to sell homes across the city in all price ranges, in all areas, to all sorts of people.

I couldn't help but notice that in case after case, sale after sale, transaction after transaction, the buyers and sellers were making the same mistakes, making the same erroneous assumptions, overcalculating and overstrategizing to the point that I became crazed, working nights and weekends to the point that I was unable to view the seventh game of the 1991 World Series between my beloved Atlanta Braves and the Twins of Minnesota.

It was then that I realized I needed to share my observations, and I sat down to write the original version of *Buyers Are Liars & Sellers Are Too!* I wrote it after having sold about 200 houses, and self-published an earlier edition that—although helpful to buyers, sellers, and my professional colleagues— lacked the depth of this revised and updated version. My editors at Simon & Schuster repaired this book the way a plumber would a leaky pipe.

Despite the original book's shortcomings, the feedback I received from buyers, sellers, and Realtors was quite positive, and they reported that many of their house-hunting and house-selling woes were vanishing into the radon- and mold-laced air. Now these usually warring parties were no longer consumed by their attempts to outthink the other guy, for buyers, sellers, and Realtors alike were armed with a weapon of mass construction. In fact, the self-published *BAL-SAT* was read across the country, and even in the Virgin Islands, Ireland, England, and South Africa: it seems that the situations I had discovered in Nashville were not exclusive to the area, but were shared by the real estate–minded in many parts of the world.

Now, 600 real estate transactions after its initial publication, I have found the principles upon which the book was based still are sound. Yes, interest rates and market conditions have changed; yes, granite-top kitchen counters are more popular than Formica; yes, the "master bath" now exists outside of old episodes of *Dynasty.* But when it comes to the basics of buying or selling a home, much of what I shared back in 1992 is still true. Now, I've updated, revised, and expanded this book to make it as useful as possible, and Simon & Schuster has joined me in this latest effort to bring peace and harmony into the world of residential real estate.

How to Use This Book

This book is designed to be used by anyone involved in buying or selling a home—whether you are a buyer, a seller, or a real estate professional representing either side. Because it unfolds chronologically as it tracks the buying and selling of a home, I suggest you read it in order, but if there is a topic that you're burning to dive into, there is no harm in flipping right to that chapter (unless you want to "flip" a property—for that, you really need to read the whole book).

I've broken down the home-buying process, from start to finish, into individual chapters. Beginning with introducing you to the Realtor and other major players like the home inspector, I'll walk you through the listing process—which includes settling on an asking price—as well as the initial house search and the showings or open house, where you'll hear all about the importance of "street appeal." You'll see what happens during the inspection, and how all this leads up to the offer, the sale, and ultimately, the closing. Whether you're a buyer, a seller, a buyer's agent, or a seller's agent, you'll find clearly labeled hints just for you in each chapter. And if you read the hints that aren't addressed to you, I guarantee you'll get some excellent insight into what cards the other players are holding and how they intend to play them. What buyer wouldn't want to know what's on the mind of the seller? And don't you want to know why the agents are giving each other funny looks at the inspection?

Finally, for those of you convinced that behind every "For Sale" sign lurks the deal of a lifetime, I'll share my views on always-hot real estate topics such as flipping and foreclosure. For several years, I've written a real estate column, "Realty Checks" for the daily Nashville *City Paper*. I'll offer some "realty checks" for you at the end of select chapters on a wide variety of topics.

The original *Buyers Are Liars* was helpful, but as the world of residential real estate has turned, it has evolved into a more complex creature. It is a mortal one capable of being conquered. This book provides you with the knowledge you'll need to slay the beast.

Chapter 1

The Realtor

No Place for Barney Fife

Remember Barney Fife, self-appointed hero of Mayberry, North Carolina? He was a man of great ambition, a man whose keen entrepreneurial mind was as finely tuned as his agile physique. Barney once saw a great opportunity to make quick bucks in the field of real estate. He saw real estate sales as one big game of dominoes.

Barney's plan was intricate and could have worked. He would sell Mr. and Mrs. Clark the home of Mr. and Mrs. Morton, who in turn would buy the house owned by the Simmses, who would then purchase the home of Sheriff Taylor, who would buy the residence of Mr. Williams. Easy enough. The deal soured, however, when young Opie Taylor disclosed some of his home's deficiencies to Mr. and Mrs. Simms.

At first Andy and Barney tried to discount Opie's observations and downplayed the home's leaks and cracks almost to the point of denial. Yes, it's sad to say. But when placed in the role of a seller, even Andy Taylor, Mayberry's finest, was tempted to lie. Andy later recanted his denial and cover-up, and was pardoned by Gerald Ford (I think). As for Barney, in his zeal to close the deal, he had breached his fiduciary duty to the Simmses and thereby proved that he was certainly not a Realtor.

Realtors are different from real estate agents. They have passed a course that teaches them ethics. They pay a bunch of money to their local Association of Realtors and to the National Association of Realtors. These memberships allow them to receive several trade magazines featuring articles concerning all the scuttlebutt in the real estate world. (Nowadays most real estate agents are certified Realtors.)

These masochists also attend luncheons and other events, and they devote their days (evenings and weekends included) to the pursuit of happiness and homefulness for their clients. Their cars are often the site of infantile vomitus explosions and other accidents. Their home phone rings at all hours of the day and night with callers wanting to know everything, such as why their interest rate is one figure and the APR (annual percentage rate) is another on a home that closed twelve years ago. Or they may even want to know the distance between the commode and the shower on their listing on Plum Street.

Or, "Why isn't the loan survey deductible? What if I deduct it? Would you write me a letter saying I can deduct it? By the way, a neighbor's tree fell in my yard and he won't remove it. Will the lawyer who closed the loan handle this for me? Free? He was a friend of yours, wasn't he?"

Some people feel Realtors are overpaid. If your Realtor doesn't earn every penny of his commission, it's your fault. Ask your Realtor questions and, more important, listen to his answers. Your Realtor knows what houses sell for in the area in which you want to buy. You must tell him where you want to buy. Make him show you comparable closed sales in the area. Ask him which lenders provide good service *and* good rates, because one without the other is useless.

Let your Realtor assist you in having a competent real estate attorney close your loan. Atticus Finch was a great killer of rabid dogs and protector of human and civil rights, and he led a wonderful crusade to save the mockingbird from extinction; however, he might not be able to prepare a deed of trust or a warranty deed or provide clear title to a property. By the same token, the lawyer who lost 600 straight lawsuits to Perry Mason might have been a wonderful real estate attorney. Unfortunately, there is not much glamour in this branch of the law.

Your Realtor will also know inspectors who know how to inspect a home rather than simply criticize it. (Of course, to optimize your home's selling potential, you may want your home critiqued, in which case that can be done, too. Your older sister is probably dying to tell you how she'd arrange the living room furniture to make the space look bigger, and your in-laws may be quite gifted when it comes to offering advice. I'll offer more constructive options for optimizing your home's selling potential in Chapter 3 "Street Appeal," and Chapter 5, "Open Houses.")

If you are listing your property, Realtors have the resources to price it, the network to market it, the expertise to aid in the negotiations, and the persistence to make it happen. And they don't make a penny until the deal is done. Make them work for it. They asked for it when they got into this crazy business.

Now, to be fair, all Realtors are not equally good. Some are mediocre . . . yes, perhaps even terrible. But most are conscientious, professional, and effective. Choose one, and choose carefully. Your selection can mean the difference between a great experience or your worst nightmare come true. You are going to eat with this person, ride in her car, have him in your home, call her at odd hours, and meet at his office. Check them out, and when you find one you like, take the plunge and stick with her. Your loyalty will motivate your Realtor to do a better job for you.

Many first-time buyers or sellers, or people who are moving into a new area, may wonder how to find a reputable Realtor. First of all, check the local papers and do some driving through the neighborhoods high on your shortlist to determine what Realtors are active in the area. Established real estate agencies are familiar with the marketplace and the quirks of a particular area, from the quality of the schools to the local shopping districts. However, by the same token, beware of the hand-off. Let's say you find an established and highly popular Realtor whom you meet and like, but then you are handed off (because this person is so popular and busy) to a subordinate in his or her office and you don't click with the subordinate. You don't need to stick with someone who gives you a bad vibe. This is an important relationship, so pay attention to your gut reactions. Remember, you will be spending a lot of time with this individual. Through the commission he will earn, you will pay for his time and insight.

If you attend open houses, tell the attending agent that you have an agent and name the agent. The open house agent won't hate you and throw you out. As a matter of fact, he will appreciate having the information, because he will know that he can call your Realtor, whom he invariably will know, and so can learn all about you without having to be nice to you.

Now we'll move into the actual selling and buying of a home, from the listing to the closing. No matter what side of the process you are on, the following chapters will better explain each aspect of the sales process.

I hope you will gain some insight as to how you would perform in your role as buyer or seller or agent, and that you'll come to understand why one skinny deputy in North Carolina had his real estate career nipped in the bud by a freckle-faced kid.

— **REALTY CHECK** —
The Top Things Some Real Estate Agents Say and Do That Drive Me Crazy

➤ *The agent says, "I am not going to let my client pay that much for a house."*

Uh, okay, who died and left the agent in charge? If the client wants the house, the agent should help. An agent should negotiate the transaction to the best of his ability and make the sale contingent upon an appraisal. Many agents do a disservice to their clients by keeping them from buying houses that eventually double in value and serve all the buyers' needs, because on that particular day that particular agent felt the price was too high.

One homeowner told me that her house had

doubled in value in only five years, and that she had fought with her agent to buy it, because the agent felt the price was too high. Only days before we spoke, that same agent had forbidden her client to make an offer on a certain listing until the price was reduced. It sold the first day on the market for asking price. The client lost because her agent flexed some muscle; no one gained. For the client's sake, I hope she eventually found a new agent.

> ### The agent insists on being present at showings.

It must sound good when the selling agent boasts that he or she will be present at all showings. Doesn't it imply a greater commitment to the listing? Well, what it really means is that the listing will be shown fewer times. Why? Because the property will be shown only at the whim of the listing agent, not when the buyer and his agent need to see it.

There are instances when a buyer—perhaps someone who is relocating and needs to find housing immediately—must make a decision on a home purchase within twenty-four to forty-eight hours. The only homes he can choose from are, obviously, those that are available within that time frame. And there's another kicker in this situation. The buyer's agent may learn, after having shown her client two or three properties, that the remainder of the houses she'd scheduled for that day's showings are not what the client actually wants to purchase (the old "Buyers are liars" syndrome; see Chapter 6, "Buyers"). The buyer and agent were not in sync when originally discussing the buyer's needs. Now the buyer's agent must start from square one, and attempt to schedule several showings over the next few hours. In those scenarios, there is no worse response to a showing request than "You have to talk to the agent directly to set up that showing, and the agent must be present." By the time the listing agent returns the call, finds the seller, and schedules the showing, the buyer has moved on to the next house on the list—one where he can actually gain entry.

The other problem with the listing agent being present is that she is, indeed, present. If the buyer feels uncomfortable being honest in front of the listing agent, frank conversation between the buyer and his agent will be stifled. Such awkwardness can lead to less time being spent in the home.

> ➤ *The agent submits a lowball offer on a property, with the flimsy excuse that the offering price is all that the buyer can afford.*

If a buyer can only afford to offer $200,000, what in heck is the agent doing showing him a property listed for $300,000?

➤ *The agent assumes the (difficult) personality of the clients.*

One reason a client hires a particular agent in the first place is that he believes that agent is better qualified than others to guide him. But when the agent starts making unreasonable demands and getting argumentative during the contract process—all in the name of representing the client—she is doing her clients a disservice. It's part of an agent's job to tell her clients when their demands are outrageous, ignorant, or irrelevant—particularly when those demands may frustrate and anger the other parties enough to scuttle a deal. Representing a client's wishes is admirable, but any true professional will tactfully let her clients know when they are out of line.

Chapter 2

The Listing

The Greatest Show on Earth

Most homeowners put great stock in that old adage, "There's a sucker born every minute," and most real estate agents seem to have a big "S" magically tattooed on their foreheads so that it appears only at listing presentations. No matter how competent or experienced the agent, the seller is determined to bamboozle him. Caution, comparable-sales information, current market conditions, and reason are thrown to the wind.

These potential sellers have decided for some reason to move, even though they are leaving the best house ever designed and constructed. The Taj Mahal pales in comparison with this place, so chock-full of amenities and representing a value so great that to sell at true market value (plus about 25 percent) entails a sacrifice assuring the sellers of sainthood.

Many sellers seem to believe this. That's when it really gets scary. I once had a client whose house, at over 2,600 square feet, had no central air conditioning. This lovely home was right smack in the middle of the Deep South. And he had chosen to sell during the time of year when the mercury hits 90 and the relative humidity likes to keep it company. He tried to explain to me how to arrange the windows, doors, and furniture to provide a draft. This was more beneficial to the human body than air generated by Freon.

Then, nobly combining generosity with environmentalism, he refused to penalize any would-be buyers by charging extra for his priceless cooling system. Yes, he would condescend to list his house for the same price as a similar house that had central heat and air. And, believe it or not, he was a reasonable man in real life.

If You're the Seller

You have decided to leave your paradisiacal palace and have enlisted the aid of a real estate agent. After much tussling, you will agree to the list price and will most likely refuse any offer that is not close to that price.

You will continue to think your home is the greatest deal in town until either: (1) ten or fifteen people have shown it, with no offers resulting, or (2) no one has shown it. At that point, you may begin to taste realty reality, although some in your position might instead blame their agents rather than accept responsibility for overpricing, market conditions, or the street appeal. If you're tired of waiting by the phone for those offers to start pouring in, consider the following.

Hints to Seller

➤ Make sure your house is clean every day. The one day you don't have it tidy, a relocating deep-pockets insurance executive with a cleanliness fetish who must buy a house that very day in your neighborhood will want to see it. Pay special attention to kitchen and bathroom areas. And don't leave embarrassing items out and about!

➤ Your cute little pet looks like King Kongzilla to some people. Your kitty makes the allergics cry like babies, or your dog conjures sad memories of a pet sent away to "live on a farm" by an evil stepfather. Remove your animal from your home when it is being shown, or have it comfortably penned. Animal lovers revolt at mistreatment. Also, anticat people loathe the look and smell of litter boxes (even if they are spotless), and you don't want some dolt accidentally letting Princess slip out the back door.

➤ Repair the little things that need it. Prior to the do-it-yourself home improvement craze, most people could not have told you whether a cracked door facing cost $5 or $500. If you lack the manual dexterity or expertise to repair the problem, please hire someone who does. It's for your own good. Legend has it that someone once dry-walled an entire room without knowing that tape is needed at the joints.

➤ If your house is shown ten times without even so much as a single offer, the price is too high for the condition or the location, and you should consider reducing it. Perhaps other houses in your area have sold for this price, but their condition must have been better. Likewise, if nearby houses in worse condition have sold for more, their locations must have been more desirable.

Trust me, if your house is priced correctly, someone will buy it, or at least make an offer. As for the offer, contrary to what most sellers think, buyers, as a rule, refrain from lowball offers. Conversely, most sellers price their home at a reasonable price. I realize the facts take away from the thrill of the hunt, but it's true.

➤ Make your house easy to show. And on short notice. If your agent calls for a spur-of-the-moment showing by another agent, don't yell. She is only trying to sell your home. Cooperate. Be gentle. Despite the nice cars they drive, agents' egos are oh, so fragile.

➤ If your agent or the buyer's agent can't be present for a showing, never try to show your home by yourself. You are not trained in this area and even if you mean well, you'll blow it. So leave!

Case in point: prospective buyers, a young couple, asked a seller if there were children in the neighborhood. The seller, noting the youthfulness of the prospective buyers, decided they must like children. "Oh yes, they're all over the place." That killed the deal. The prospective buyers hated children. No kidding. As it happened, the area didn't have any more or fewer children than other areas that the prospective buyers were considering.

➤ The buyer's agent is not trying to "sell" the listing. He is guiding prospects through potential homes. It is the buyer's choice. Don't expect your agent to try to sell the buyer's agent.

If You're the Seller's Agent

You have already made a listing presentation to the seller in order to gain the listing. This presentation usually includes a Comparative Market Analysis (CMA), which details the most recent sales in the area, the homes that are currently listed, and any sales that are pending. This report is actually more valuable than an appraisal, which would cost several hundred dollars.

Appraisals generally compare only three sold properties. Rarely has an appraiser seen the interior of the comparable sales. On the other hand, if you, as the seller's agent, are active in the area, chances are good that you have shown (or even sold) most of the homes in the CMA. You will then price the new listing accordingly, if the seller will listen.

Important: Note the "Days on Market" category of the CMA, which a real estate agent will know, but which an appraisal will not indicate. Highlight this information for the seller. A house comparable to hers may have sold for a great price, but what if it spent seven years on the market first?

Hints to Seller's Agent
➤ Keep in touch with your seller.
➤ If you agree to list the property at a price that is

too high, remind the seller in writing that you feel it is too high. Sellers have a tendency to forget they insisted on the price in the first place, and then blame the listing agent when their home doesn't sell.

➤ The property is your listing but, more importantly, it is the seller's home. Respect that.

Finally, try to follow up on showings and report back to your client, but explain in advance why it may not always be possible to do so. As you may know, many times the seller's agent will not receive feedback from the buyer's agent, and with good cause. In some cases, buyers are forced to purchase homes within a one- or two-day period for any number of reasons.

In those cases, the buyers sometimes see as many as ten or twelve houses in a day. The buyer's agent is driving them around the area all day. That evening, the agent will prepare an offer and begin negotiating it—while also attempting to return twenty or thirty phone calls and a hundred e-mails. Imagine that ten or twelve of the messages are inquiries from you as to how the buyer felt about your listings.

The feedback is this: if your client's house is not the one getting the offer, the buyer did not like it. Feedback from showings is usually worthless. Suppose the buyers needed an extra bedroom. Is the seller going to construct one? What if the buyer needs a nine-foot ceiling to accommodate a piece of furniture? Will your clients raise the roof?

Most houses are not for everybody, but every house works for somebody. Remind your client that it is important to make her home easy to show—meaning easy for the buyers and their agent to gain entry any time, day or night. If only one person out of forty will like the house and that person is denied admittance, then the sale will require forty-two more showings. Prepare your seller to wake the child, crate the dog, and take a walk.

If You're the Buyer's Agent

The buyer's agent has many ways of monitoring new listings in order to arrange for the Greatest Showing on Earth. These include driving through his areas and noting new signs, listening to word of mouth (or networking), and monitoring listings electronically through the Multiple Listing Service (MLS). The MLS is an invaluable information source, whose members are able to input and retrieve data for every property that is currently on the market or that has closed within the last year.

This MLS information is much more timely than any information that might be retrieved from the office of the Register of Deeds because the member users of the MLS enter sales data immediately following the closing, whereas it could take the closing attorney a week or two to record the transfer. (We'll discuss this more in Chapter 4, "Non-Agent Listings: For Sale by Ogre.")

Buyer's agents communicate with seller's agents in establishing their great showings. They try to give the listing agent as much notice as possible before they show a property. However, it is not uncommon to stumble across a property in the midst of showing other homes. Perhaps the listing is new, or the place looks better in person than it does on screen. During these times, the buyer's agents may call the seller's agent and ask to show the property on fifteen to thirty minutes' notice. It is important for the seller to comply with these wishes, because the prospective buyer may not return.

Hints to Buyer's Agent
➤ Please make every effort to contact the listing (seller's) agent so that they can report news and activity to the seller.
➤ Tell the truth (I know it hurts). If the property is overpriced, tell the seller's agent. The agent wants to know—or, more probably, needs an excuse to tell the owner (seller) the perception of an unbiased person.

If You're the Buyer

Ideally, you are being shown properties that your agent feels you find interesting. The seller (property owner) may not always remember that you aren't familiar with the history of the property and probably don't care about it, either ("This is where my husband was standing when he got his big promotion"). That said, if you find yourself being dragged down memory lane by a seller, complete with bad decor, don't forget to look past that history to see a property's potential.

Hints to Buyer

➤   Try to imagine the house as if it were furnished with your belongings or painted differently. If the decor is horrible, the house won't sell quickly, and you might be able to purchase it at less than market price. Many ugly houses have potential to be better than the spick-and-span, dolled-up, freshly painted sizzler homes.

➤   Tell your agent what you like about each home and what you do not like. Be truthful, thoughtful, and specific. For example, don't tell her you hate all frame houses if you hated one particular frame house just because the wood was painted chartreuse. If you do, you will not see another frame house with that agent. Then, when you buy a pretty frame cottage from another agent because your original agent couldn't find anything you wanted, you will be remembered forever as a liar. And you *will* see your original agent in the produce aisle someday.

— REALTY CHECK —
Getting Your House in Order

In my experience, buyers are often repulsed by a home's decor, personal memorabilia, and condition. They can't look past these details to see the potential of the property. Home sellers can take a few simple steps to neutralize these hot spots and make a buyer feel welcome.

Just as the number one rule in small talk is to avoid discussing religion or politics, the same should be applied to home decor. As the country has become more polarized, both liberals and conservatives have increased their public displays of affection for a particular cause or candidate. A diehard Democrat touring a home featuring autographed pictures of Ronald Reagan and George W. Bush might spend less time viewing the residence than trying to figure out how to convince the seller to vote her way. A career army officer might be offended walking through a house decorated with peace symbols, "Wage Peace" signs, and autographed pictures of Chairman Mao.

However, the most often repeated crimes against neutralism are perpetrated by cigarette smokers and cat owners. Cigarette smokers will argue that they never smoke inside and that no one could possibly find the faint scent of cigarettes offensive. But I have had numerous buyers take one step into a house and cry, "A smoker lives here!" Then they bolt out the door.

Cat owners feel there is a bias against their fuzzy friends; however, the bias is actually against urine and feces. Who cares if it's all wrapped in a fine coat of sand? The non-cat person thinks, "I would not use a litter box for dogs. This disgusts me." So, if you must have the litter box available because you haven't removed your animal temporarily during the showing, at least put the contraption in an inoffensive, discreet location. And make sure it's absolutely odorless and cleaner than your own bathroom (which should border on sterile).

You've got your cat (or barking dog) under control, but what about your middle schooler or teen? Celebrity posters of sports or music figures abound among the youth of today, introducing a new wrinkle in adolescent decor. Some kids have them plastered on the walls; many of their subjects are scantily clad or imaginatively tattooed. While some potential buyers may be able to look past this wallpaper job, they may still wonder: Does this poster cover up a crack in the plaster? A nasty nail hole? A gash the size of the Grand Canyon? Work with your child to reduce the clutter in his or her bedroom, and hope that your potential buyer has a kid the same age.

What about religious paraphernalia? While no one should abandon his faith in order to sell a home, religious displays fall into the same category as political ones. Neutralize. Put the religious para- phernalia away. Make your statement discreet, if you must make one at all. (Of course I've had clients call upon their religion to help them in the sale, some by burying a St. Joseph statue upside down in their backyard, others by dancing around a bonfire in a toga. But just keep it to yourself until after the closing.)

Incidentally, my own house smells like dogs and I have a fine vintage of French's mustard (1996) aging in the refrigerator. My Tennessee Titans flags dangle merrily over my "Cooper for Congress" sign and the numerous Beatles photographs that dot the walls. However, my home is not for sale.

Most Realtors agree, "Less is best." Remove darn near everything from your home that is not used on a daily basis. Clear counters, empty closets, eat everything in the fridge, take the canned goods to

Second Harvest, and scrub the whole joint from top to bottom, inside and out. Send the pets to the in-laws and make the children clean their rooms and wear surgical gloves.

See you at the closing.

Chapter 3

Street Appeal

The Grass Is Always Greener . . . on the Lawn of the House That Sells

By definition, all home showings begin with the exterior of the property. Unless buyers are to approach and enter the house blindfolded, the exterior view is a logistical reality. Therefore, first impressions are very important, whether you're a buyer or a seller.

This first-impressions theory seems obvious, but I have spent hours in debate with my buyer clients, while sitting outside poorly landscaped homes with neglected lawns and enchanting interiors. During these debates, I have used all my persuasive skills in an attempt to make prospective buyers release their seat belts and join me in a promenade through the home. Many times they wouldn't even get out of the car.

If You're the Seller

No one knows your home the way you do. If you love your home, you've molded and shaped it into a place that gives you great pleasure. You eat here. You sleep here. Why, you truly live here.

Sellers sometimes have quirks. One seller I know carefully and regularly wipes away any condensation that forms inside his refrigerator. Let's just say he has a thing about water droplets. He was irritated when an agent had the audacity to wash his hands without toweling off the droplets of water from the inside of the homeowner's sink when he was finished. Yet this same seemingly meticulous homeowner saw no reason to waste water on a lawn or something as worthless as a holly bush. The result? The well-kept (droplet-free) interior of his home was very inviting, but his environmentally correct watering practices killed his lawn and nearly killed the sale of his home.

Hints to Seller

➤ Get the exterior perfect. Landscape. (That's a verb.)

➤ See above. Paint. (Also a verb.)

➤ If there is anything hanging (a downspout) or banging (a shutter) where it shouldn't, get it fixed.

➤ Work with your agent in prioritizing exterior and interior repairs and the expenditures within your budget. An expenditure of $200 in one area may have a return of $2,000. However, $200 spent to repair an item that has annoyed you during your stay in the house may not return a nickel. Be smart. That'll be the day your house value skies.

If You're the Seller's Agent

You can tell when a home needs exterior work. That said, you may be reluctant to tell a seller how you really feel, for fear of not obtaining a listing. But if the property lacks street appeal (also called curb appeal), you will be tremendously handicapped in marketing the property.

Before you take a listing, be honest with the seller. Be tactful and practical if you are offering a critical assessment of the property. Any criticism you make should be followed with a constructive remedy or solution. For instance, don't just say, "This kitchen could use some updating." Instead, say, "You should consider repainting the kitchen and changing the countertops from laminate to granite. I know that's not a minor expense, but based on the comparable sales in this area, you could really increase the value of your home with a change like that. I honestly think it would be a good investment."

Many potential buyers prefer to drive by a property before making an actual appointment to see it. They feel an appointment is too much of a commitment. If a residence lacks physical sizzle, buyers will not go in, no matter how hard the buyer's agent tries to persuade them.

Hints to Seller's Agent

➤ If landscaping is the big issue, have an artist draw a rendering of the home with landscaping in place. (Note: The seller should agree to the cost of items such as an artist's rendering.)

➤ Ask your client nicely and tactfully to make the changes you've suggested. If that fails, beg.

If You're the Buyer

Your first inclination is to judge the book by its cover. As I mentioned earlier, when I've pulled up to the front of less-than-stunning listings, I've had to pry fingers loose from car door handles just to get my client to walk past the dead sycamore tree and into the light-filled den and gorgeous new kitchen. Most buyers want to buy a house that will allow them to drive home, call all of their friends and family, boast about the beauty of the new place after announcing the street address, and gloat over their business savvy in negotiating a great deal. You don't want to be embarrassed by your purchase when family and pals see the outside after doing the inevitable drive-by. Image. Pride. Ego. Whatever you want to call it, it's there and it's understandable. But it's also worth setting aside.

Hints to Buyer

➤ Swallow your pride. If the neighborhood is right, if the house has "good bones," this could be the deal of a lifetime. (See Chapter 14, "The Deal of a Lifetime.")

➤ Even if you don't want the all-committing "appointment," ask your agent for an information sheet and learn whether the number of bedrooms, room sizes, and appliances are within the realm of your wishes. If so, go see the darn thing.

➤ However, beware! An improperly maintained exterior can lead to severe structural problems. That'll be the day the house makes you cry.

If You're the Buyer's Agent

You want to find your client a home she will be proud of. If she's really resisting all listings that show poorly from the outside, don't keep pushing. Avoid

arguing with a client over whether she should purchase a specific house. Ruffling a buyer's feathers can
lead to the buyer looking for a new realty henhouse.
Buyers want direction, but very subtle direction.
They are the ones who have to live with and in their
home purchase.

Hints to Buyer's Agent

➤ When showing a dump that could be a Shangri-
la, have an architect or draftsman draw some
rough sketches and secure ballpark estimates from
contractors for these alterations. (Make sure your
client agrees to the cost of this step in advance.)

➤ If you are showing a home that has been
renovated, try to obtain before and after shots,
and share them with your prospects. If they
don't buy that particular home but show an
interest in renovation, you may find them
increasingly open to properties that need TLC.

— REALTY CHECK —
Home Is Where the Chi Is

A recent visitor to an open house commented to me
that there was incredible feng shui in the kitchen.
Having attended one too many Led Zeppelin con-
certs, I don't have the hearing I used to, and the term

"feng shui" did not compute. After checking my shoes to be sure that I had not stepped in the shui, I wandered into the kitchen to see whether the homeowner was perhaps serving a gourmet Chinese buffet.

When another person mentioned feng shui, I consulted with Andy Lee, the owner of Nashville's Chinatown Restaurant, and knower of all things Chinese. He quickly pointed to the two bird statues that adorn his front window. Chinese decor? No. It's feng shui, pronounced "fung shway." Andy offered a quick lesson in this increasingly popular practice that Americans and other westerners are now incorporating into their dwellings.

In the restaurant's parking lot there are three telephone poles. Applying feng shui principles, Andy felt the poles symbolized knives that could stab him in the heart, robbing him of happiness and wealth. So he put the birds in the window to combat these knives. One cannot argue with his rationale, for many businesses in the same area have folded their unfeng tents, while he has prospered for years.

The term "feng shui" translates as "wind and water"; feng shui is the ancient Chinese art of placement or energy flow. The energy that feng shui harnesses is known as chi. Mary Shurtleff, a feng shui expert from Draper, Utah, explains that "chi must flow unobstructed within a home to produce a happy, healthy environment."

Now, what does this have to do with house-hunting or home-selling? It turns out that good Realtors are shuists of the feng variety. For instance, like Andy Lee and Mary Shurtleff, most Realtors shun clutter. Clutter can shrink a room more quickly than a king size waterbed. Clutter creates negative chi and impedes the flow of positive energy. So get rid of those stacks of unread magazines. Toss out the pyramids of old yogurt containers, even if they are clean. Declutter and organize the tops of desks and coffee tables, and weed out the bookshelves if they are packed to overflowing. Hunt down and neutralize the piles of shoes, athletic equipment, and shopping bags that lurk in many a home's entryway, not to mention those unsightly piles of unopened mail. And don't forget the exterior of your home: if you're trying to maximize its street appeal, remember that those plastic toys or gardening tools scattered across the driveway and all over the front lawn are the equivalent of clutter.

Sharp angles should also be avoided; they are referred to as "poison arrows," which will poison the energy, unless of course, they are neutralized. So, if the decor is sharp and pointy, buy some round-leafed plants—maybe even a very round Buddha—and place them in front of the angles. Are you starting to get the idea?

All houses have a floor plan. In order to incorporate feng shui into the home, a "Ba Gua" must be implemented. The Ba Gua incorporates the Eight Aspirations, which are career, self-knowledge, family, abundance, fame, integrity, creativity, and benefactor. At the center are health and good fortune. If the Ba Gua is improperly or disproportionately planned, the lives of the inhabitants will be out of kilter.

According to Mary Shurtleff, Feng Shui is similar to acupuncture: if an organ is overworked, pins are inserted to slow the rate of its function; if an organ is dormant, the pins stimulate it. The yin and yang principles are similarly applied in feng shui. A person would want the bedroom to be on the yin side—that is, with no mirrors, with soft colors, perhaps with some still water to slow the energy. The yang requires more energy for the family room and kitchen so that the inhabitants are not transformed into couch potatoes.

Andy Lee suggests that a person should not purchase a home at the end of a cul-de-sac. The wealth will follow the road around the cul-de-sac and into the home of a neighbor. (And if you currently live on a cul-de-sac and have always found the guy next door highly annoying for some indescribable reason, now you know why.)

Whether you're buying, selling, or settling into a home, if you yearn for more yin or yang or feng or shui, you can find information in numerous books and websites, including Mary Shurtleff's website, www.designwisdom-fengshui.com.

Chapter 4

Non-Agent Listings

For Sale by Ogre (I Mean, Owner)

Though I am a real estate agent (a Realtor, no less), at one point in my life, I decided to delve into a non–real estate venture. To partially fund our new endeavor, my wife and I decided to sell our house. My real estate license was still active and I was a member of the MLS (Multiple Listing Service); however, I was not active in the real estate community. We listed our home for sale, with my firm's broker as the listing agent. Why? We needed money. We needed to sell our home and retrieve the equity. We needed to net as much as we possibly could.

We hired a Realtor and agreed to pay him a 6 percent commission, even though I had my real estate license and access to the MLS. I could have "for sale by ownered" it, plus one notch better. But my wife and I had other jobs and we couldn't afford the sales time and effort needed to net the best results. We needed a person with his finger on the pulse of the marketplace.

We were told it would be foolish to list our house for over $89,000, though I had wanted to list it for $110,000, hoping to net $100,000. Ultimately, after researching the area, the firm agreed to list it for $99,000 with a new agent who had "nothing else to do." However, a second firm had talked to us about listing our home, and agreed to list it for more—$116,000. They ultimately sold it for $106,000. So the moral of the story is, get more than one opinion. Even if you're a Realtor.

As it turned out, my wife and I bought three houses and sold four during the next two years by using a Realtor, when all the while I had an active license and was a member of the MLS. Our agent earned his commissions, and my wife and I earned handsome profits—simply by heeding his advice.

Who, then, would try to sell their houses themselves? Answer: people who don't know any better.

If You're the Seller

An owner-seller is often referred to as an FSBO (pronounced "fizzbo"), for "For Sale by Owner." These people view real estate agents' car phones, sales awards, and offices as scalps on poles or notches on the grip of an old-time gunslinger's six-shooter. They see agents as money-sucking leeches who put a sign in the yard and wait for the check, or as underpricing con artists draining unsuspecting homeowners of the equity in their homes.

FSBOs say that agents don't give them any value for the improvements they have made on their homes. Most FSBOs want to recover every penny they have ever put into their house—even expenditures that would usually be considered matters of maintenance. (Lawn care, painting, decorating, and roof repair are not investments in your home.)

It's also ironic that these misers, who are trying to save a real estate commission, have overspent in almost every aspect of the home. They have a six-ton heat and air system when four tons would have worked. They paid $4,000 for ten shrubs and some monkey grass.

What's more, the sly dogs painted the house themselves. It only took them six weekends and twenty-eight weeknights, sixty gallons of paint, ten brushes, four dropcloths, three paint pans, five ruined suits, and a stained carpet. And everything's a different shade of purple. (The owner saw it on *This Old House*. She failed to note that the featured home was a 1908 Victorian in downtown Baltimore, while she and her husband live in a 1958 ranch in a Mid-western suburb.)

Many homes become FSBOs because the sellers had several real estate agents give them comparative market analyses and found that their home was not worth what they had hoped. So what do they do? The same thing Barney Fife did. They become real estate agents. And what usually happens? The same thing that happened to Barney Fife: their career is nipped in the bud. But not without a fight! Ogres can be very, very stubborn.

Hint to Seller

➤   Get an agent.

If You're the Seller's Agent

In the case of FSBOs, seller and seller's agent are physically one and the same, yet psychologically they are worlds apart. Think of the seller's agent as volatile Mr. Hyde, with calm Dr. Jekyll being the seller. When showing his home, Mr. Hyde is unable to tol-erate the criticisms that unwitting prospective buyers utter when they forget for a moment that the seller's agent is, in fact, the seller himself.

Fizzboing ogres can attack without warning, usually convincing the potential buyer to call an agent immediately rather than deal with an ogre. For that reason, ogres are usually great at generating business for agents. Their homes can't be shown except during off hours. And usually these showings aren't really showings at all. They're more like tours with a sales pitch—in fact, the hardest sales pitch you've ever had laid upon you.

"What's wrong with our home?" the ogre fizzboes.

"No den," the prospective buyer blurts.

"Whaddya mean no den? We use *this* room as a den," the fizzbo ogres, loudly.

"But it has a stove, a dishwasher, and a refrigerator in it. It's a kitchen!"

"It's not a kitchen. It's a well-equipped, functional den. Very user friendly, especially if you want a snack!" the agenting owner counters.

"We're outta here."

Hint to Seller's Agent (aka Mr. Hyde):

➤ Don't fizzbo. Get a full-time agent.

If You're the Buyer

As a buyer, you may have heard that FSBOs are bargains. After all, you're saving the real estate commissions, right? Oh, but you had to pay some lawyers

$200 an hour to write contracts, which may not even go through. (You might recall that buyers' agents usually receive compensation only when the sale closes, and that most of the time, the seller will pay.)

What about a loan? You'll save those costs with a FSBO deal, right? FSBO buyers generally go to their banks to get their loan. And why not? After all, that's where they have all of their accounts. But what they often don't consider is that a bank's mortgage department may not even be in the same state. They usually pay more for the loan than if they'd had an agent.

And what about accountability? What if the seller sort of fudges about those "old" watermarks on the basement walls or about the new apartment complex being built in the backyard? One couple I know once tried to save an $1,800 commission. They had heard they should buy FHA (that is, with a Federal Housing Administration loan). The seller told them they would have to pay him $2,000 extra to go FHA. "It's normal," he dishonestly claimed. They paid asking price plus $2,000 for a house that he told them had "about a thousand" square feet. If 800 is about 1,000, then he told the truth. So what? Could they call their state's real estate commission? No. He wasn't licensed. Could they complain to the National Association of Realtors? No. He's not a member. Could they sue him? Not easily, since they used his lawyer.

Hint to Buyer

➤ Get an agent.

If You're the Buyer's Agent

There are times when agents must don their ogre armor and venture into Fizzboland. It's never fun, but their clients deserve it. When all other options have failed, the agent can begin negotiations with the ogre. It is more difficult than dealing with other selling agents, because MLS information is Greek to an ogre.

Ogres are determined not to pay a commission. They are proud to a fault, and they have drawn a line in the sand. However, the agent can and usually will prevail.

Hints to Buyer's Agent

➤ Assure the ogre that you are merely an agent for a potential buyer; you're not an enemy.

➤ Explain the offer in a thorough, noncondescending manner. Remember: you have done this every day for years, while the ogre is trying to remember the next step in the real estate book he bought to assist him in this sale. He has never seen an adversarial agent in person. He has never negotiated a deal. Still, the ogre possesses a large ego, which needs massaging. Remember: ogres can be transformed into humans. After all, they do have to move somewhere. Tame them, and they can be yours.

— REALTY CHECK —
Words They Didn't Teach You in School

You are no doubt already familiar with some common real estate terminology such as "mortgage," "for sale by owner," and "money pit." Here are some additional and sometimes arcane terms that Realtors like to toss around, demystified for your use.

Annual Percentage Rate (APR) Especially during the closing, this is the one that raises the blood pressure of any borrower. Although the Realtor and the closing attorney attempt to thwart the borrower's cardiac arrest with professional banter as the relevant contract page outlining the APR is presented for signature, borrowers attest to the fact that sound travels more slowly than light. Furthermore, the buyer will always be confused by the lender's math. For example, a loan with a fixed rate of interest at 5.5 percent could have an APR of 6.876 percent if there is prepaid interest and a discount point or two. Nobody ever gets this one. Accept it.

Closing The closing is when the transaction is closed. At that point every contingency in the contract evaporates. The voluminous lady sings. There is no going back.

Commission The meager amount paid to the real estate agent for his or her role in the dramatic play that was the sale and purchase. The seller pays for this more times than not; the fee is negotiable, and usually paid at closing, only after all the work is done. In some limited-services firms, the commission is paid in advance and referred to as a fee, and is paid regardless of the success of the agent's efforts.

Comparative Market Analysis (CMA) This sales analysis is compiled by someone other than an appraiser—often, by a Realtor. A CMA is a list of all of the active, pending, and closed listings in a specific area similar to the house in question. This data provides information that can be helpful in determining the value of a house.

Deed of Trust A deed of trust secures the lender's interest in the loan. In Tennessee (and in some other states), we use this instrument, commonly referred to as a mortgage. In short, it states that if the borrower defaults on the loan, the house will go into foreclosure and will become a great deal for people who watch those cheesy "get filthy rich in real estate" in-fomercials at two A.M.

Mortgage Loan Inspection The most important doc-ument in the universe, according to some. The mort-gage loan inspection results in a map formally known as the loan survey; this map informs the buyer of any encroachments that might exist on the property. In some cases, the buyers' driveways have been poured on neighboring land, or the neighbors on either side have inadvertently encroached on the buyer's new piece of property. This encroachment, which should be resolved before final closing, could involve fences, swimming pools, garages, dog runs, ratty old swing sets, and pink plastic flamingos.

Chapter 5

Open Houses

Where Woodward and Bernstein Lurk, While Ida Dunn Offers Commentary

ellers view open houses as the magic bullet. Homeowners who go the open-house route have visions of people lining up outside their front door as if Springsteen tickets have just gone on sale inside. It usually doesn't happen that way.

Woodward and Bernstein wannabes are usually the first on the scene, attempting to discover the fraud perpetrated by the sellers and their agent in a conspiracy to sell this potentially defective dwelling for such a high price. They come armed with beguiling, open-ended, and innuendo-filled questions.

For example: "Why is that vanity placed that way in the half bathroom? Is that up to code? Why are there carpets everywhere? Are they covering a defective floor? Why are the owners moving? Is there something you're not telling us? We've been told by an anonymous source that there's a carton of expired milk in the refrigerator."

These real estate sleuths are followed by the elderly Mr. and Mrs. Ida Dunn. They are not looking to buy, just getting ideas in case they move. The Dunns have lived in the same house for sixty-two years and paid $6,000 for 4,500 square feet. They can't believe the shortcomings of this place.

"I mean, this is all right, but you know what Ida Dunn? Ida put the shelves on this wall and the fireplace on that wall."

"And that hot jaccyousa. Heck, it's outside. Who in their right mind would ever take a bath outside? I tell you what Ida Dunn. Ida put that tub in the bathroom where it belongs."

Many times the Dunns and the Woodwards and Bernsteins gang up on the agent and make for a long, long afternoon. Know what Ida Dunn? I wouldn't have that open house until I was ready to deal with party poopers like them.

If You're the Seller

Many sellers—that includes you—view the open house as the end of the sales trail. You can't imagine that the visiting tire-kickers could find your home anything other than irresistible. Perhaps you circle the outside of your home from a discreet distance during the open house, gleefully noting the model of each car that stops and imagining the career and income of each Woodward, Bernstein, and Dunn. You may make bets on which person will make the highest offer. After a while, you get bored with standing on the curb and go to someone else's open house. If you're really feeling cocky, you interrogate unsuspecting real estate agents and tell them how fabulous your home is compared to this one, and offer helpful hints on what you'da done.

When it's all over, you can't believe that more people didn't attend your open house. Nor can you believe the agent didn't sell your home after you spent days cleaning and getting it ready.

Hints to Seller

➤ If you have an open house, make it no less than perfect. Clean, declutter, then clean again. Talk to your agent about ways to "stage" your home to make it as desirable as possible. (See "Realty Check: Getting Your House in Order," on pages 21–24 for more ideas on how to make your house more inviting and presentable, inside and out.)

➤ Do not expect a miracle. Most listed houses are sold as a result of scheduled visits by other agents.

➤ Open houses are not a panacea. If agents are not showing the home, there are two possible reasons: (1) they don't see it as desirable and are not recommending it to their clients; (2) their clients don't feel the home is one they would like to see. Open houses do not cure overpricing, lack of street appeal, or any other shortcoming.

If You're the Seller's Agent

Your primary responsibility is to sell the house you're holding open, even if it's a tough sell. Some prospects will wander into the house and simply hate it, loudly deploring every aspect. If you can engage them in conversation, ask them light-heartedly if they have friends who might love a house that they, themselves, abhor. Listen pleasantly to their objections and don't argue. They're not going to buy *this* house, but with some effort, you can convert them into your buyers. They may have a house to sell and will appreciate the good humor and energy you exerted on behalf of the faulty open house. You will be more likely to gain their respect—and their listing—than will an agent who either argues with them or joins them in enumerating all the shortcomings of the open house.

Hints to Seller's Agent

➤ Have something open as often as possible. Doing so will keep you in touch with the buying market and provide you with feedback on your listings.

➤ Let your other clients know where your open house is when you have one. That way, they will realize you often do work seven days a week.

➤ Communicate. The "C" word, once again. Yet it's what most of us do worst. Before the open house, help your seller present his home in the best possible light. Offer specific suggestions for readying the property, from cleaning and repairs to decorating. Or bring in a third party to help stage and get the property ready, if your client is open to paying for this increasingly popular service. After the open house, let the owners know what happened.

If You're the Buyer

Hopeful buyers should attend as many open houses as possible. Open houses offer a free, leisurely view of the active market, they educate you about house styles and features, and they provide you with a hunting ground for finding real estate. You may also find the agent you will use to sell the home you live in now.

Many buyers use open houses to confirm a decision made during the previous week. Their agent has shown them several houses and they have decided to begin negotiations over one. In order to reassure themselves, they tour the area.

Hints to Buyer

➤ Tell the agent at the open house your reason for being there.

➤ If you have an agent, inform the attending agent immediately upon your arrival. This can avert problems later.

➤ Remember things you liked and things you found distasteful. You may have an open house of your own soon.

If You're the Buyer's Agent

As an active agent, you will probably wind up hosting open houses on the same days that your buyer clients are on the prowl without you. Unfortunately, it's impossible to be with your clients at all times. Even the best agents have seen clients duped by the less virtuous members of the real estate world, and lost a sale while a client bought a clunker.

Buyer's agents are confident they have shown their clients the best there is and represented them as well as possible. The thought of innocent buyers out on their own is terrifying. The fear isn't so much about losing commissions or wasting time invested, though a little of that is natural and healthy. Rather, you worry that the buyer will make a mistake that you will have to work hard to undo—or even worse, that he may purchase an atrocity that you will some-day have to sell.

Hints to Buyer's Agent

➤ Give your clients dozens of your business cards and ask (beg) them to offer them to the agents holding open houses. That little piece of cardboard will send a message: your clients are spoken for, and when it comes time to negotiate, your job is to speak for your clients.

➤ Call your clients following their open house tours to see if they did anything in which you need to become involved.

➤ Pray that Woodward and Bernstein don't meet Mr. and Mrs. Ida Dunn. If they wind up having a confab in loud voices in the front hallway, they're sure to turn off or alarm some prospective buyers, which they—clearly—are not.

— REALTY CHECK —
Another Opening, Another Show

If you are in search of entertainment on a Sunday afternoon between two and four P.M., consider a visit to an open house. If you situate yourself near the person hosting the event, be she a real estate agent or a FSBO, chances are you will overhear a plethora of questions, most of which are relevant.

How old is the roof, or the HVAC (heating, ventilation, and air conditioning system)? Is the plumbing copper or galvanized? Is the electrical wiring knob and tube? The answers to those questions will assist the buyer in working out how much money must be budgeted for maintenance.

But the most frequently asked questions, which I like to call the Magnificent Seven, usually have no relevance whatsoever to the price the seller will accept for the house. Yet, Sunday after Sunday, buyers feel these questions will provide them with information relevant to preparing their offer.

1.   Why are they selling? Unlikely answers: they invested all they owned in Enron, or they have learned their home is built over a long forgotten nuclear reactor, which has only recently cracked and begun to pour radioactivity into the crawl space. It does not matter why they are moving.

2.   What did they pay for the house? The seller may have paid too much, or too little. Most often, the buyer paid the market value at the time of the purchase. Hint: if the property appreciated 5 percent per annum over a six-year period for the seller, chances are it will appreciate 5 percent per annum over the next six years for the buyer. Buyers hate for sellers to realize a gain or, dare I say it, a profit. Profits are good. Losses are bad. Buy a house that has appreciated.

3.   How long has it been on the market? It is hard to believe, but veteran real estate agents will agree that length of time on the market may not be a factor in what a house sells for. Thousands of properly priced (key words) homes have been on the market for hundreds of days, then receive multiple offers on the same day. Don't let DOM (days on the market) be a factor in making a low offer. You could lose the deal.

4.   How much do they owe? If a person owned $150,000 in stocks and owed nothing on the asset, would he sell it for $135,000? There must be an obscure theorem that states that unencumbered real estate should sell for under market value. The theorem does not hold true for the transfer of any other asset, of course.

5.   *What is the tax appraisal?* With all due respect to your town's assessor, that office is probably unable to inspect and appraise every parcel in your region, unless it's a very tiny region. Disparities between tax values and market values have greatly lessened over the past few years (much to property owners' chagrin). However, tax appraisal is not the line on which to hang your real estate wash.

6.   *What's the square footage?* Much ado about nothing. It's not the feet, it's the shoes. What's covering the feet? Nine-foot ceilings or eight-foot? Crown molding or not? New kitchen, old kitchen?

7.   *Have they had it inspected?* Maybe, but so what? Any buyer needs to have the home they buy inspected by their own inspector.

So, if you're not busy this Sunday, hit an open house or two. And you can cross the Magnificent Seven off your list of questions and enjoy the show. Or come up with some really good, juicy, relevant questions of your own.

Chapter 6

Buyers

It's a Good Buy
or It's Goodbye

B uyers. You gotta love 'em. They know everything. They know exactly what they want to buy and exactly what they want to spend. The only problem is, they speak a language called buyerese that is a variation of liarese.

Liarese is the language of liars, a group of people who at times distort or twist the truth, usually for their own benefit. Buyerese, however, differs significantly from liarese, in as much as buyers are really *trying* to tell the truth. For some reason, though, when people begin looking for a house, the truthful needs and impulses swimming around in their vast neurological ocean somehow don't flow over their vocal cords. To the untrained observer, it would seem that these people are liars. But they're not really liars—at least, not on purpose. They're simply buyers.

I have some dear friends who returned to our hometown of Nashville after having lived in another city for several years. He's a lawyer and she's an architect. It might seem that they wouldn't require a real estate agent because, between the two of them, they should know everything. Nevertheless, they couldn't find the house they wanted, so they asked me to assist them in their search.

At our first meeting, they laid out their criteria. They had a young child, so they didn't want to be on a busy street. As a gauge, they ruled out any property on a street with a double yellow No Passing line. She had designed a number of homes and was partial to frame construction, although brick would be considered. They did not want stone. They refused to live on a corner lot. They wanted all the living area on one floor and they did not want to spend over $125,000.

It was obvious to a person schooled in buyerese why they had been unable to find their dream home. They were speaking buyerese and didn't know it.

Where are they now? They are happily settled in their new home. It is a beautiful one-and-a-half-story stone house with a basement (three floors)—comfortably situated on a corner lot bounded by a street with a double yellow line. And they paid $126,000 for it.

If You're the Buyer

Once they get past the language barrier, sellers find that buyers really are good people. And some buyers actually do, in fact, know what they want. Many buyers think they know what they want, but really haven't approached enough houses from a buyer's perspective to be able to contrast and compare the multitude of possibilities.

As a buyer, you may initially feel intimidated. You are swimming in uncharted waters, armed only with horror stories from friends and bits and pieces of information garnered from newspaper articles, late-night television promotions, and a how-to book (not this one!). You may get so distracted by all this "advice" that you may find yourself unable to differentiate between a well-built, nicely designed, functional, but messy home and a clean, shiny, meticulously organized, structurally nonfunctional dwelling. You may worry more about roof color than roof condition. And common settlement cracks will scare you to death. At first. But you need to hit the streets and get the hang of looking at other people's houses, with an eye toward making one of them yours.

Hints to Buyer

➤ Begin your hunt with an open mind. Cull as

you go. Unless you're a veteran house hunter, allow yourself to be schooled by a trustworthy agent and the realities of the marketplace.

➤ Try to remember why you want the things you do. The reasons may be trivial.

➤ Explain to your agent why you don't like a particular house you visit. Be specific, so that the agent can rethink your needs and wants. On the flipside, if there is something about a house you absolutely love, speak up.

➤ There's no reason to be embarrassed about changing your mind. After seeing several homes, many people realize that they were completely wrong about what they wanted. Change is good. You are going to have to live in your house. You're going to have to write the checks. Tell your agent.

➤ Never lie or speak buyerese. If you can't stand a particular home, tell your agent (even if she is the one listing it).

➤ Don't be afraid to find the house you want. When you find it, buy it—even if it's the first house you see. Now, this advice may fly in the face of what first-time buyers are frequently told: don't buy the first house you see. But if you truly love the first house you see, and it's priced right for you, then go for it. If you're more cautious, go ahead and look at more houses after that, but be aware that the first one—especially if it's a great buy—may vanish quicker than you can say, "Let's drive back there and look at it one more time." I've worked with many a client who loved the first house she saw; all the properties she saw afterward paled in comparison. In some cases, that first house is still waiting for the buyer after she feels she's seen enough listings. But often it's gone, and the disappointed buyer can't shake the feeling that she's settling for whatever she winds up with (even if it's a fantastic house). Nothing is ever as good as the one that got away.

If You're the Buyer's Agent

Normally, a potential buyer is referred to an agent or vice versa. The agent then meets with the buyer to establish his financial capabilities, a process sometimes called prequalifying. (I fail to see what's so "pre" about it.) Using the financial profile provided by the buyers, the agent determines what they can afford. They then define, to the best of their abilities, their dream home.

As the buyer's agent, you are just that . . . an agent. You are not going to pitch any homes. You will run a CMA to learn whether they can afford the kind of house they want. You will point out benefits and features of such a home or neighborhood, as well as deficiencies. Price range often eliminates some areas, and the agent must then search the remaining areas for homes that meet the standards set by the prospective buyers.

Next comes the showing mission. The first few days are devoted to reconnaissance expeditions that familiarize the buyer with the territory and natures of the beasts in the realty wilderness. Then the short list is made. At this time, spouses or significant others join the fun, if they haven't piled on already. When the dream house finally emerges from the pack of listings, pencils are sharpened, ballpark figures for financing turn into estimates, and magnifying glasses appear. The word "contract" (gulp) is used.

Hints to Buyer's Agent

➤ Listen.

➤ Translate what buyers are saying into what they mean. Be thorough with your comparable sales and financial representations.

➤ Don't be afraid to give buyers a subtle push if they find the right home. Sometimes they're begging for it.

➤ Keep 'em happy.

If You're the Seller

The buyer is your friend. The buyer is the person for whom you have waited and toiled. Every person who sees your home is not a buyer. There will be only one. Every home has its good features, along with several characteristics that might put some people off. Most homes have flexibility but are not structural chameleons, able to change to suit the lifestyle of every person. So when that buyer comes along, play nice.

Sellers should not talk to the buyers before the closing. Even if you have good intentions and are trying to "help" the sale along, every word may be held against you at a later date. Realize, too, that if prospect traffic is good through your home, but no buyer surfaces, the house is not a good buy.

Hints to Seller

➤ If you priced your house too high in hopes of gaining an unusually large profit and the house hasn't sold in two months, reduce the price. When you reduce the price, put a "Reduced" sign on your "For Sale" sign, and note this fact in any ads or flyers that are in circulation. Otherwise, John Q. Public will be unaware of the reduction. It does not reflect a "fire sale" attitude on your behalf. The price is reduced. The house is for sale. Let drivers-by know it.

➤ Try to view your home objectively. Clear your mind, drive to a real estate office, and then drive back to your home and pretend you are a prospective buyer. See how it looks as you approach and how easy it is to enter. Sticking locks or squeaky, inoperable doors suggest more inoperable things to follow. Walk through each room as you would someone else's home. View it through a visitor's eyes. Open your senses. Sniff. Are there any strong and distinct smells in your home? If so, whether it's perfume or last night's fish sticks, neutralize the odors: they will not appeal to everyone. Trust your nose. It knows.

A sound analogy: in the multimillion-dollar recording studios in Nashville, after all the tracks are laid and engineers have spent hours upon hours getting each note of every instrument and each voice mixed perfectly while listening on zillion-dollar sound systems, they flip a switch to see how the song will sound on a cheap car radio. That is where the decision is made. The song must pass the test of the keen ear of the engineer, but the not-necessarily keen ear of the consumer is what matters most.

The same applies to your home. The little

details are great, but don't forget the basics. If your house smells, your neighbor's sells.

If You're the Seller's Agent

The seller's agent must work with the seller to make the property as easy to show as possible. The property should be priced competitively, be easy to show, and be free of any petzillas or reminders of them, as well as free of glaring deficiencies. Reread the first half of Chapter 2, "The Listing," for a quick refresher on this topic. As the seller's agent, you must cooperate with other agents and agencies in the sale of the property and use every resource available to transform prospects into buyers. You will arrange the showings, open houses, inspections, contract negotiations, appraisals, and closing. Only then do you get paid.

Hints to Seller's Agent
➤ Make the property showable.
➤ Make the property sellable.
➤ Make the seller negotiate.
➤ Work it till you drop.
➤ Make it a good buy or it's goodbye.

— REALTY CHECK —
The Changing Face (and Rates)
of Today's Mortgage

In the early 1980s, interest rates for home loans were hovering at about 18 percent for 30-year fixed mortgages. For those who are unaware of current financial trends, as of this book's writing, interest rates are at about 6 percent. In the 1980s, as rates rose to catastrophic highs, home sales and new home construction declined to the lowest levels since the Great Depression.

Thanks to the staggeringly high interest rates, homeownership became the American Nightmare rather than the American Dream. Monthly payments were prohibitive for the average person. For example, a $100,000 loan at the 1981 rate of 17 percent requires a monthly payment of $1,425. The same loan amount at 5.85 percent (the 2003 rate) would have a payment of less than $600.

On the basis of financial ratios established by the Federal National Mortgage Association (FMNA, or Fannie Mae), a 1981 borrower would have needed an annual income of $60,000 in order to afford a $100,000 loan. In 2003, an income as low as $21,600 would enable her to afford the same loan. The person making $60,000 today qualifies for a loan of $275,000.

As home sales diminished in the early 1980s, new construction followed suit. Ancillary industries that support the building industry began to erode financially. Sales of building materials plummeted. The rapid rise in the rates during the 1980s was unexpected and created a situation with which the country was unfamiliar. Seemingly overnight, carpenters, plumbers, architects, and contractors—along with all the other home-building tradespeople—were out of work. Therefore, their ability to purchase goods and services vanished. The automotive industry soon felt the chill that would eventually freeze car makers, with the sales of cars and trucks slowing to a virtual halt. Quite simply, when Americans stop buying houses, they stop buying automobiles. When those two industries collapse, financial mayhem follows.

In an effort to save the free-falling housing industry and the economy as a whole, bankers, Realtors, and governmental policy makers convened to devise a new financing mechanism that would return homeownership to affordability. As a result of their collaborative efforts, the adjustable-rate mortgage (ARM) was born and introduced to the home buying public.

By the time ARMs were introduced, the interest rates had dipped to a whopping 15 percent. However, with an ARM, the buyer would be allowed to purchase a home with a first-year interest rate of 11 percent. Returning to the $100,000 loan model, the payments dropped from $1,425 to $952. A person making an annual income of $34,000 could buy the same house that would have required an income of $60,000.

The borrower takes a gamble, inasmuch as the loan adjusts on a specific day. In some cases, the day can be an aberration on which the rates spike for those 24 hours, and the consumer is locked in for the next twelve months (see Chapter 11, "Little House on the Variable"). Interestingly, a large number of loan officers have their personal residences financed on ARMs. To judge by the interest rate swings of the last fifteen years, they have backed the right horse.

Recently, a new product has entered the market that offers an incredibly low interest rate (in 2003, it was a mere 3.87 percent). This is an interest-only loan and its rate is based on the London Interbank Offering Rate, or LIBOR. According to John Stephenson, a mortgage specialist with World Lending Group, the interest-only loan originated in Europe because of the exorbitant prices of property there. Again, using the $100,000 loan model, the payment with the 3.87 percent LIBOR rate would be $315. Therefore, payments have dropped from $1,425 per month in 1981 to $952 per month in 1983; and then from $600 fixed rate in 2003 to $315 on the LIBOR—all for the same amount.

The LIBOR is adjustable, and remember, it is interest only. After a defined period, the borrower has to start paying the principal and the rate generally increases. When considering a mortgage, a borrower should compare apples to apples. Lending institutions offer a cafeteria-style array of products. Be aware. Be informed. And watch those rates.

Chapter 7

The Parent Trap

Ma and Pa Meddle

Before they finalize the purchase of their home, many buyers—especially first-time buyers—want their parents to inspect the property. The buyers have not heeded a word of advice from their parents since they were eleven years old, but now, following twenty-odd years of arguments and disagreements, they want the folks to share in the biggest decision of their lives.

Personally, I would prefer an inspection team comprising Felix Unger, Frank Lloyd Wright, and Sherlock Holmes, especially if the parents are divorced. The "see who can find the most wrong" game begins.

The parents have not lived with their children since the kids were in high school. They think their kids still leave their retainers on the sink and pop pimples onto the mirror. It follows, then, that they must know exactly what their children want and need to fit their Neverland lifestyles.

It's even more alarming when the parents are unfamiliar with the market. They are astounded at the prices and, oh, the interest rates! The amount of the monthly payment elicits expressions of shock, pain, and disbelief. How in the world can their little boy or girl afford such an expense? The poor kid makes barely $2 a day selling lemonade on the corner! Most parents in this situation haven't shopped for a home in over twenty years and can't fathom a thirty-year mortgage. All that interest!

And don't let the parental eyeglasses fool you. They are just a prop. These wonderful people can spot a nail hole from seventy feet and through two sets of windows. They can hear a floor squeak at a noise level otherwise audible only to bats. Not only that, but they are upset with the real estate agent for trying to make their children spend more than they can afford, while repaying an exorbitant loan at usurious interest rates on an overpriced property.

If the property is newly constructed, the old adage "They sure don't make them like they used to" is always heard. As for older properties, the saying is

"Son, you could get a brand-new house for less than they want for this old thing."

Generally speaking, however, the real problem is that parents want the best for their children, and their children simply can't afford the best. No one wishes they were buying a bigger home more than the Realtor does, but facts are facts, and this is it. Parents are not shy either. The "Have you seen this?" cry usually echoes down the hallway at least five times, prompting a race to the source of the utterance. Usually the great horror turns out to be a very minor defect—say, a leaky faucet.

If You're the Buyer

You may feel your parents are better qualified to make this decision, since they have done it before. Never mind that their homes were purchased when an ARM was just an appendage attached to the shoulder. Building codes were more relaxed in the past and deficiencies were grandfathered in. They *don't* make them like they used to. Of course they don't. It's illegal!

But it's normal for you to want Ma and Pa to approve—just as it was when you brought home your prospective spouse for the first time. Your parents, of course, never thought anyone would be good enough for their little darling, but eventually they came around. Well, get ready, because they're gonna pull the same number with the house.

Hints to Buyer

➤ Honor thy father and thy mother . . . after you buy the house. Honor thy agent and thy inspector and thy own good judgment first. You're the one who has looked at seventy-two properties trying to find the right house. You've had your agent work her tail off and run the comparable sales and the mortgage numbers, while shopping rates from California to Sweden. The inspector has donned his coveralls and crawled over, under, and through every inch. Your parents, bless their hearts, are just standing there.

➤ Give your folks a hug, put them in their car, smile, and wave. Walk back into the house and sign the contract.

If You're the Buyer's Agent

You've done everything you can for your client, but now your work is at the mercy of highly subjective, usually underinformed persons. Still, you must present only the facts and not appear to be determined to make the home pass this particular inspection. Additionally, you must reinforce your client's decision to purchase. Comparable sales quotations, financial information, and references to any inspection that might have been performed should be shared with the parents (assuming the offspring wants you to do so).

In short, Ma and Pa must be provided with all the information Junior had when he made the decision. Forget that you have spent sixty hours with the potential buyer, have years in the business, and have done hours of research in order to get the deal to this position. You still must share all your accumulated knowledge and data with the parents in thirty minutes, while not appearing biased. It is a challenge that approaches the impossible, but this too shall pass.

Hints to Buyer's Agent

➤ Let Ma and Pa meddle. They're an unstoppable force of nature.

➤ Reinforce their ideas when these are accurate. Thank them for their insight in areas you might have missed, and admit you missed them.

➤ Correct the parents (gently, gently!) when they are wrong, and always do so respectfully. Even if they haven't purchased a home since the Watergate era, they probably have maintained one longer than you have.

➤ Roll with the punches. Thicken your skin. Smile. You can scream in private, later on.

If You're the Seller

You're so close to selling. By now you may feel you have been persecuted and tormented throughout the months the house was on the market, beaten up during contract negotiations, and wrongly accused by an inspection. And now! Now you have to hope your house appeals to people who will probably visit it two or three times a year for the next six years. I have never seen "subject to parental approval" as a condition of a contract, but it might as well be.

Hints to Seller

➤ Leave the house and go look at the place you're moving into. The deal's going to work out, despite Ma and Pa.

➤ If you can't help but spread the misery around, have your own parents inspect the house you are buying. If that's not possible, borrow the parents of one of your friends. It has the same effect.

If You're the Seller's Agent

As the seller's agent, you have done everything required to get the situation to this point. Now you must do everything necessary to overcome this predictable ob-

stacle. With any luck, you've seen enough parental inspections to know how to advise the seller (if not,
check in with a trusted, more seasoned colleague), and
you can work with the buyer's agent to determine if
any pre-parent preparation should be taken.

Hints to Seller's Agent

➤   Have the home accessible for elderly people. The
     parents are usually in better shape than I am, but
     sometimes age makes for physical limitations. Be
     alert and sensitive to any special needs.

➤   Ask the other agent if you need to be present for
     the parental showing, but make every effort to
     avoid attending. Two agents can seem like a gang.

➤   Give them the key and let Ma and Pa meddle.
     There's no stopping them, but ultimately they'll
     realize the whole family will be happier when
     their child has her own home (and is no longer
     at risk of turning into a freeloader who moves
     back into her childhood bedroom).

— REALTY CHECK —
Terminating Termites, Not Your Contract

Homeowner wannabes sit anxiously in closings
awaiting the delivery of the feared and revered "termite letter." Upon its arrival, the closing attorney

peruses the familiar verbiage and informs the buyers of the exterminator's findings. If the letter is "clear"—if there was no evidence of active infestation—the buyers breathe a sigh of relief and the closing continues.

If, however, there is evidence of active infestation, the closing attorney will send for the defibrillator, as cardiac arrest will quickly ensue. As the buyers writhe and moan in agony over the diagnosis, they begin the process of deciding whether they want to buy the now stigmatized home.

The fact is that buyers should want the termite letter to reflect that the inspector actually found termites. This is because most real estate contracts require treatment if there are termites or other wood-destroying insects present. A "clear" termite letter means that no termites chose to rear their ugly heads, set their cute little wings in motion, and fly into the face of the representative from the pest control company. There are termites present in every property.

According to the Department of Agriculture, the United States has about twenty-five termite colonies per acre. Therefore, on a half-acre lot, there could potentially be twelve colonies with upwards of a million termites or eggs per colony. That adds up to approximately 12 million termites on an average lot.

Now for the good news. Termites are not an endangered species. They can be killed legally, and that's why legions of pest control companies are in business. A termite is an insect that can lead a charge into a home and consume most of the lumber within a matter of hours. To label this insect as a pest is a bit of an understatement. Fleas are pests. Termites, to most homeowners, are more on the "axis of evil" level.

Throughout the 1970s, 1980s, and 1990s, termite letters were merely a formality. The contract called for a "clear" letter, and the pest control companies were quick to oblige. Only on rare occasions were termites observed. Today, the opposite is true. If a house is not under a treatment plan, nine times out of ten, termites are present.

Anyone who buys a house should contact a termite control company immediately after closing. It should be the first call you make, even before you change the utilities. Cable television is worthless if the television is buried under a heap of sawdust and termite droppings. The power of a swarm of termites is awesome. They can destroy the framing of a room in a house in a few hours. They are a stealthy lot, chomping voraciously but silently.

Before entering into a contract with a pest control company, the consumer should confirm that the company will be responsible for repairs should the treatment fail. In some contracts, the company agrees only to treat the property again if the termites invade but is not liable for repairing the damage done during the assault. The consumer should enter into an agreement only with a company that will repair the devastation left in the termites' wake.

There are various types of treatment. The EPA outlawed DDT, a chemical that took all the sport out of extermination. DDT treatment is like fishing with dynamite. Everything dies: termites, rats, snakes, dogs, and people. This was biochemical warfare before it came into vogue. Fortunately, there are now environmentally friendly chemicals, including one called Termidor (www.termidorehome.com, for more information), which can differentiate between termites and mammals. Happy house—and termite—hunting.

Chapter 8

The Offer

The Greedledees Meet the Greedledums

The sellers have called their agent repeatedly, begging for action. They really need to sell their home. They are moving, or they have found the perfect home. Bring them an offer . . . any offer. Make somebody do something.

The prospects who saw the sellers' house loved it. It has everything they could ever want and more. The price is right. Interest rates are right. Venus is aligned with Mars. This deal should be simple to put together, right? Wrong!

This is where the Greedledees meet the Greedledums. Davy Crockett had it easy at the Alamo, compared with what's in store for these combatants. But it doesn't have to be that way.

If You're the Buyer

You have looked at many, many homes. You have defined and redefined your goals. Of all the places you have seen, this one is the best. You knew the price when you walked in. Your agent has supplied you with a CMA that should establish its value. You have slept on the decision, prayed over it, read the tea leaves, run the numbers, put a pencil to it, and asked Ma and Pa. Now you have only one more question. You just can't help it. You feel that you have to know:

"What did the sellers pay for it?"

"What difference does it make? They bought it over thirty years ago," the agent says, reasonably.

"We just wonder."

"They paid $12,000."

"And they want $97,000?"

Never mind that $97,000 is actually a very reasonable prize, to judge by comparable sales. Never mind that it is better suited for your needs than any home currently on the market. You have just met the Greedledees. I hope you are not looking in the mirror.

In an effort to try to make your partner enter the realm of realty reality, the less greedy of you asks: "What do you think they have in it?"—meaning, what is the monetary value of the improvements the sellers have made to the home? You hope this amount will be $35,000 or more. That way the seller will be, at best, breaking even, and maybe even *losing money.*

The mere thought of a seller taking a loss brings a gleam to the eyes of the Greedledees. (Certainly you are above this, yes?) They clasp each other's hands. They want to boast of their financial conquest to Ma and Pa. ("Look, Ma, no hands!")

Yes, the Greedledees want blood! They will not sleep if the seller is able to sleep. (By the way, the Greedledees met their agent at church.)

"Let's offer $50,000," the Greedledees grumble.

Now would be a wonderful time for a recitation of the Beatitudes or the Golden Rule, or even a simple: "Why the heck did you even look at homes in this price range if you're going to offer this?" But patience is a Realtor's virtue. So he will offer you the following nuggets of truth.

Hints to Buyer

➤ What the seller paid for it is of little consequence.

➤ What the seller "has in it" is of little consequence.

➤ A horribly low offer will not save you money or get you a deal. In fact, it will probably cost you later.

➤ Prioritize. If price is your main concern, avoid

nagging (pointless) contingencies such as a certain interest rate, securing specific employment,
or a child's acceptance in a private school. Neither the buyer nor the seller has control over
those conditions; therefore the offer has no
strength. Or, if price is not your priority, add as
many contingencies as you like. (For example,
your offer may become contingent upon obtaining a certain type of financing, or on allowances
for repairs related to structural problems,
HVAC, electrical wiring, or plumbing.)

You can catch more homes with sweet, reasonable offers than you can with sour, lowball ones.
Don't be a Greedledee.

If You're the Buyer's Agent

You have spent hours setting appointments and
showings for your clients, researching every angle,
and basically tending to the whims of the Greedledees. It seemed odd that they were looking for a
$100,000 home when they dressed in garage-sale
clothes, but nevertheless their financial situation jus-
tified it. They seemed so subdued and congenial during the various showings.

Hints to Buyer's Agent

➤ Beware of wolves in cheap clothing.

➤ Use comparable sales, this book, or anything you can to get the first offer into the nonabrasive zone.

➤ Warn the other agent and beg for a counter.

➤ Don't try to justify the unjustifiable. If your offer is too low, do not try to convince the other agent that the property is overpriced.

➤ Warn your buyers that neither the Constitution of the United States nor the Bill of Rights nor any other amendment guarantees individuals "the right to negotiate."

➤ Give your clients a chance to get a good deal by offering a reasonable interpretation of their requests. If they feel they should offer a lower price than you think the seller will take, offer it anyway. Who knows? Maybe the seller won the lottery that morning. However, the buyers should be instructed that fewer contingencies, large earnest-money checks, and a convenient closing date translate into a good deal.

If You're the Seller

An offer is a piece of paper. It cannot harm anyone. If it is too low, a counteroffer should be made. No one has to accept an offer. There's no reason for anyone to become overly angry or upset. The offer is a start, and it's better than what was there prior to the offer.

Unfortunately, many sellers see the offer as a line drawn in the sand or a call to battle stations. A war is on. They morph into Greedledums. They want asking price. ("This house is perfect. It's better than the one down the street that sold for less.")

The offer is the first step toward attaining the goal set when the house was put on the market. And yet the offer is often unappreciated, even despised.

Hints to Seller

➤ The buyers think they have a constitutional right to negotiate. Give it to 'em. Don't be a Greedledum.

➤ Remember the CMA and your agent's initial visit. If the agent is suggesting you take less than the CMA, point that out to him. If you are getting what the agent projected, accept it.

➤ Try to purge unnecessary clauses and conditions, such as those irrelevant contingencies mentioned earlier. When negotiating counteroffers, reduce everything to specific amounts of money. Rather than squawk over possession dates, for instance, determine the cash required to allow one or the other party to rent for a period, and ask for the money instead of arguing over who will move in where on which day. Rather than debate the accuracy of the inspector's suggestion that the outlet in the bedroom, the sink in the bathroom, the shingles on the roof, and the tile in the mudroom need repair, convert the tasks to money.

➤ The potential buyers may not be much, but they're all you've got right now. Try to keep the deal alive.

➤ If the buyers offer to pay you for your house, you aren't "giving it away."

If You're the Seller's Agent

The sellers have bemoaned the lack of an offer for days, weeks, sometimes months. As their agent, you have tried every trick in the book to get even a nibble. Yet, when a fish finally takes the bait and you bring an offer to the seller, things change.

The sellers can't imagine why you are so excited. "Whose side are you on? This offer stinks! If it were cheese, it would be Limburger." The sellers want to make it Swiss. All this talk of food has made them hungrier still. They decide to keep their stove and refrigerator, even though they already have a matching set in the basement and another pair in the garage. The Greedledums are staying home. Maybe for good.

Hints to Seller's Agent

➤ Separate the contract into sections; important, unimportant; affects their net, doesn't affect their net; normal conditions, abnormal conditions.

➤ Remind them of the CMA.

➤ Give them a chance to get a deal. Counter and test the water (if it's within realty reality).

➤ Represent the best interests of your clients even if they don't agree with you.

Warning to Greedledees and Greedledums

John Lennon wrote and recorded a song titled "Instant Karma." Most listeners are unaware that it's about real estate. If you greedle, "instant karma's gonna get you." If a Greedledee becomes obsessed with hurting the seller and greedles him to the point of no return, the seller will eventually refer the 'dee to another piece of real estate—the pavement.

If the Greedledee has not negotiated in good faith, instant karma occurs. That Greedlebuyer will never, ever see a deal as good as the one that he let greedle away . . . and the seller will get a better offer than the Greedledee's.

Likewise, instant karma can hit Greedledums. If they greedle would-be buyers away, the buyers will 'dee-terminate. In layman's terms, they will not be back, and the Greedledummies will never see an offer as good as the one they refused.

If you are a buyer and you fail to reach an agreement with a seller because of his Greedledumness, fear not. Instant karma is with thee always. You will get an even better deal down the road.

— REALTY CHECK —
Turning the First Offer into a Final Sale

Most real estate veterans preach the importance of negotiating the first offer into contract status. For those unfamiliar with real estate jargon, an agreement for the purchase of real estate is only an offer until both sides agree on all conditions, at which time it becomes a contract. That contract can include numerous contingencies that must be satisfied in order for the transaction to be completed, but it is a binding contract.

Yet going from "offer" to "sale" usually doesn't happen without considerable back-and-forth. Just as many buyers are hesitant to purchase the first home they see, many sellers refuse to sell their house to the first person to make an offer. If the offer is reasonably close to asking price, the seller feels she priced the house too low, a sentiment shared with every human who listed a house. If however, the offer is low, the seller is irritated to the point of insanity. In order to save sanitariums from overcrowding, sellers should consider a lowball offer merely a few drops of ink smeared over a sheet of paper. It takes sticks and stones to break the sellers' bones; the words (and numbers) should never hurt them. Sellers should be prepared to negotiate, as should buyers.

In the case of early offers, sellers feel cheated that more potential buyers were not dazzled during the viewings. Others feel the whole thing is a conspiracy, that the agents colluded to have the house sell at a price substantially below the market. (They also know that Neil Armstrong never set foot on the moon, but rather stepped onto the sandy floor of a movie set.) Sellers should remember that there is nothing wrong with an early offer—it just means someone really wants the house.

By far, the most prevalent mistake sellers make is in being confident that all buyers expect a counteroffer. General Robert Neyland, a successful football coach at the University of Tennessee from 1926 through 1952 (with breaks for military service), once said that when you attempt a forward pass in football, only three things can happen . . . and two of them are bad. Neyland's wisdom transcends football and can be used in real estate. When a seller counters a buyer's offer, only three things can happen, and one of them could be catastrophic: the buyer can accept the counter; the buyer can counter the counter; the buyer can reject the counter and walk.

This is certainly not to say that the initial offer should always be accepted, but even strong first offers are rejected at a high rate. Contrary to popular belief among sellers, most buyers do not make offers in order to initiate a protracted, emotionally draining negotiation. They just like the house and really want to buy it for a fair price. When a buyer presents a reasonable offer that should be accepted and instead it is countered, that insults him. Many buyers—particularly those who make strong, good first offers—do not expect a counteroffer. In some cases, counteroffers can be counterproductive.

The wise among you will consider those first or early offers and work them to death, rather than automatically reject or counter. Stifle those knee-jerk reactions and take the first step in negotiating a fair deal: listen to the other side. On many occasions, the offer that seems to have no hope eventually reaches contract status.

Chapter 9

The Sale

The Sacrificial Lamb

Both buyer and seller have greedled to their hearts' discontent. They have described each other in language that would make Lenny Bruce roll over in his grave. They have insinuated that their agents are carpetbagging weasels. They have forgotten the reason the entire operation was undertaken in the first place: the sale of a piece of real estate.

Both parties have countered and recountered and re-recountered and decountered. They have decided that they love things they formerly abhorred, and that they could care less about things that seemed so dear to them only hours ago. Suddenly, in a gesture that would make Mother Teresa seem selfish, one party accepts the counter of the other. Only to be nice. Not because it is a good deal. Not because the other party has negotiated in good faith and sacrificed a great deal. And certainly not because either agent has done anything of merit.

Rather, it is because the acceptor is the redeemer, the chosen one, sent by a higher power to bestow riches upon the party of the second part. Hallelujah! The counterers also feel that the counter they proposed was a bit too high, but for the good of the world of real estate, they have offered themselves as a living sacrifice.

When the appropriate Greedle accepts the counter-counter-counter, there is no joy in Greedle-ville. You see, now they know one thing for sure: They offered too much. Hence the real estate agent's paradoxical dilemma: Greedledees think that if Greedle-dums accept their counter, then they countered too high. Greedledums think if the 'dees accept their counter, they countered too low.

But if neither party accepts a counter, there is no sale. So one Greedle must make the ultimate sacrifice. It is a far, far better thing than they have ever done before.

If You're the Buyer

You cannot believe you are paying this much for that house. The price is higher than you promised yourself you would go. (You didn't mean to, but you even lied to yourself. What evils hath realty reality wrought upon you?) You tried to convince your agent, too, that you would not go above a certain price.

But oddly enough, the house was listed for more than your preset amount, and you still couldn't wait to see it. You even called the listing agent in case your own agent was unable to drop every single thing to let you see this wonderful prize of a home. Sadly, I've known buyers to insist that they wouldn't pay more than, for example, 90 percent of the listing price, even if the house was priced perfectly.

Many times buyers lose the home of their dreams over a couple of thousand dollars, which in buyer's terms equates to $17–$24 a month for the length of their residence, which is usually less than seven years. (That's $1,800 spread over eighty-four months.) Tsk. Tsk. Instant karma's gonna get them.

Hints to Buyer

➤ *Carpe dealem*. Seize the deal. Fight for the best deal on the best house. When the right one comes along, don't mess around.

➤ "Pride comes before a fall"; so say Lennon and McCartney in "I'm a Loser." Don't stubbornly refuse to negotiate or to go higher because you feel you're above all that. I've known buyers to lose houses for amounts as small as $500.

➤ "Instant karma's gonna get you." Don't treat the seller like chopped liver.

➤ If the house will appraise for contract price, you have not paid too much. If you have a financing contingency, the house must appraise.

➤ "Don't worry. Be happy" (Bobby McFerrin). You really will find a seller who will sell to you, and you'll get your new house.

If You're the Buyer's Agent

Suck it up, because you're about to become the least appreciated player at this point of the game. As the buyer's agent, you have shown your clients thousands of square feet of construction and acre upon acre of land. You have exhausted every resource available, from the multimillion-dollar Multiple Listing Service to the 75-cent area newspaper—in an effort to represent the buyers as efficiently and effectively as possible.

Now, buyer (Greedledee) and buyer's agent (you) have agreed that they have found the right place. They have made an offer and a counteroffer. They have danced around the real-estatic floor. But here comes the latest counteroffer, and the deal is at risk of stalling and dying. Now you must become the heavy. Even with the counteroffer, the deal is a good one—the equivalent of hitting the sweet spot in the tennis racket. Yet, to the buyer, it is still the ultimate sacrifice to accept the counteroffer.

Hints to Buyer's Agent

➤ Arm yourself with data. Not only data about comparable sales, but, more importantly, data about current market conditions. If there has been a shift in the market, past sales are not as important as current sales. In a volatile market, check pending sales and same-house sales (i.e., the prices of houses that have resold recently). In a hot market, a review of sales of six months ago has no relevance and buyers can lose houses by offering a price based on past sales. If a market is trending downward, a buyer could overpay. Check with the local association of Realtors as to current trends.

➤ Conjure and evoke memories of homes less attractive. Remind the buyers, gently, that the market in their price range is limited.

➤ Appreciate the buyer's position. Be nice.

➤ If it is a good deal, say so. Real estate is your profession.

➤ Remind the 'dees that $2,000 is $2,000 to the seller, but only a few dollars per month to them.

➤ Thank them for their sacrifice.

If You're the Seller

You placed your home on the market, never dreaming of the inconveniences, hard work, and embarrassment involved. Your home has been invaded by these ETs (equity thieves) during every hour of the day. Then some ETs return for a second visit . . . and a third. Then they want to bring their parents. (Don't believe it? Go back to Chapter 7.) "These prospects must love the place! They'll pay anything!" the Greedles among you begin to dum. All this work will finally (and literally) pay off, you think.

Then comes the offer.

And thus begins the War of the Worlds. After a valiant effort, the Homelings realize that the advanced weaponry of the ETs is too formidable for their protective shield, i.e., their agent. So they surrender. Chances are, they received more than the CMA projected, but it's an empty, hollow victory.

Hints to Seller

➤ Prepare for a battle with the ETs by arming yourself with hard facts like current market data, specific comparable sales, and a list of improvements you have made. Be reasonable and limit that list of improvements to impressive, tangible items, such as an all-new heating system or a brand-new roof—exclude items that fall under general maintenance, like painting, landscaping services, or having the chimney cleaned.

➤ Take the second best price for the CMA if it is actually comparable to your home and has closed within the last ninety days. Use that price per square foot as your goal.

➤ Play to not lose, not to win. Then you won't and you will.

If You're the Seller's Agent

You have had an open house, networked with other agents, mailed fliers, advertised in newspapers, buried a statue of St. Joseph, placed the home in the MLS, and done all kinds of other things to bring this moment to pass.

This buyer is the one. No one else in the whole, wide world wants the house at this point. The sellers need to sell their house for a fair price. Still, the sellers suggest that you are out for a commission, not their best interests. Hogwash! Reputation is more important than any individual sale.

Hints to Seller's Agent

➤ Let the sellers say five mean things to you with-

out debating or defending. On the sixth, defend
your point.

➤ Make the sale happen. The first offer is usually
from the eventual buyer. Keep it alive.

➤ Don't expect thanks. They usually don't come.
But you should still count your blessings.

— REALTY CHECK —
Moving On Up

When a sales contract is finally executed, many
buyers and sellers seem to get tripped up by possession date—when they can actually move out of the
old place and into the new one. Typically, a buyer
can't wait to stuff his new garage with his old junk,
while the seller can't seem to assemble a single
packing box.

Each side feels it should be given several days to
move, while finding it incomprehensible that the oc-
cupants of the property into which they are moving
cannot vacate prior to closing. "We just need to
move a few things in early." How about a piano,
three dogs, a sofa, and forty odd boxes? All this is
complicated by the fact that in many real estate
transactions, buyers are also sellers, and vice versa,
unless someone is moving into or out of a rental
property where they may have some flexibility, or the

buyer is the first occupant of a new-construction home, or the seller has kicked the bucket and doesn't need to move anywhere.

A new ritual seems to have come into vogue, the rite of moving. It is an ecumenical celebration, lasting a bit longer than Hanukkah but not as long as Lent. It seems to involve quite a bit of clothes-rending, gnashing of teeth, and pouring dust over the spouse and children. This ritual does not involve the cutting of grass. As a matter of fact, it forces its practitioners to abstain from any sort of yard maintenance once the contract is signed, except, of course, for the removal of all flowers, fruits, and vegetables.

Buyers participating in the rite of moving are required to drive by their future home on a daily basis and take note of any activity in which the current owner is involved and report their findings to their Realtor immediately. If the grass is not cut and continues to grow, this must be reported. In the summer months, when rain is scarce and heat is abundant, buyers want their future lawn watered, even if they aren't yet picking up the tab on the water. However, the seller is involved in the rite of refraining from watering the yard.

Meanwhile, the sellers feel they are being sucked out of their homes as if by a tornado and being forced to watch all of their belongings being broken by demons dressed as moving company employees. They moan and writhe in frustration as the buyer's furnishings are piled upon their own furniture.

Somehow, closings finally occur and houses are in fact cleared of the former owners and their stuff, except for the stuff they do not want anymore. As a housewarming gift, sellers often leave buyers small, nasty tokens of their appreciation for having pummeled them throughout rite of moving. Perhaps some Campbell's Chicken Noodle soup. Circa 1956. Maybe even a set of Niagara Falls shot glasses, one featuring the Flying Wallendas as they tightrope across the falls. (Bright note to buyers: it's all yours now—some of these left-behinds could be worth something on eBay!)

It seems simple enough to solve the problem and avoid the consequences of the rites (and wrongs) of moving. Sellers can begin packing shortly after contract execution. As the closing date nears, they should accelerate the packing accordingly. Then have several movers prepare bids and describe their services; choose one. The movers arrive on the closing date and pack their van. After closing, the movers take the van to the new house and unload. There is no reason, contractual or otherwise, why these pesky but necessary moving tasks should not be performed simultaneously. The physical task of moving is no fun, especially when small children, furry animals, and years' worth of accumulated give-away piles fill the closets. But remember, the door prize makes it all worth it: a brand-new house to call your own.

Chapter 10

The Inspection

The Dealslayer

Ma and Pa have meddled. The Greedledees have greedled the Greedledums. The ETs (equity thieves) have pillaged and plundered the ogres. Ida and her old man have Dunn the house in and Woodward and Bernstein have tongue-depressed their deepest throat. It is now time for the inspector.

The inspector arrives with a flashlight, coveralls, a ladder, and a clipboard equipped with a form that lists all the possible deficiencies of a house. The form also has a disclaimer stating that the house could fall into the earth two seconds after the inspector's departure and that he can't be held accountable because, after all, he's just an inspector and is therefore unable to see into the future.

Some home inspectors hate houses and attack them with a vengeance, noting every settlement crack, nail pop, paint chip, and squeaky faucet. They may note a cracked plinth block on the report, or even a crack in the flitch beam. Flitch beam. Plinth block. It's all Greek to the buyer. One buyer might freak over a cracked plinth block, while another might not flinch at a cracked flitch. Plinths are decorative. Flitch beams are structural. There is a huge difference.

The buyer should educate herself as to what is major and what is not in a home inspection. Do a little research beforehand. Ask your Realtor what to expect. A nice Q&A with the inspector while your Realtor is present is a tremendous opportunity to gain knowledge. It is also an opportunity to establish who—buyer or seller—should be responsible for what, if there are any repairs to be made. However, remember that the inspector has not read the contract, nor does he have any experience in negotiating contracts. Many an inspector has quashed a good deal by overstepping his bounds, confidently indicating who should shell out cash for what. Also, by noting meaningless trivialities, the inspector may cause the buyer to fail to register a real problem. A few home inspectors feel they are there to slay the dragon (with the deal being the dragon).

An inspector may have been a builder in another life during which no one bought his spec houses. He may have a vendetta against real estate agents. And some inspectors simply like to scare people. Remember when you were little and people told ghost stories? Some home inspectors tell house stories with the same motive. Others try to impress you with their keen knowledge of construction, engineering, and even areas that don't pertain to houses—for example, international finance, European culture, and extraterrestrial life.

Good inspectors arrive and ask questions before providing answers. "What am I looking for?" or "What are your concerns?" With an understanding established, they will point out what they see—either huge problems or minor flaws that the buyers might want to address at some point during their occupation of the residence.

The best way to find a good home inspector (who should be licensed, of course) is to ask your Realtor. She has participated in numerous inspections, both as a buyer's and a seller's agent, and will know the tough guys, the slouches, the doomsdayers, and the factslayers.

If You're the Buyer

You are scared to death that you're making a mistake, right? Fear and dread are perfectly normal. Few of us can write a big fat check and sign a binding contract without some anxiety. Buyer's remorse is a very real psychological state that most buyers will experience. Therefore, the inspection provides a monumental opportunity for relief, satisfaction, and justification. Your homeful hopes hinge on the outcome of this perilous exercise performed by a total stranger. No doubt you will believe every word the inspector says and even some he does not.

If the inspector says, "The roof looks like it's about five or six years old," you may not realize that means it should last another ten or fifteen years. What you hear is: "The roof is old and must be replaced immediately." You also may conclude, without doing any research, that the cost of a new roof is much greater than it really is. The same fears will seize you when the inspector comments on something that may be scary or mysterious to you, like a furnace or a foundation. But don't panic—just speak up and ask some questions.

Hints to Buyer

➤   The inspector is the expert. You are not supposed to know anything about construction. If the inspector says something that you don't understand, ask for an explanation. You're paying for that information. Watch him work and pay attention. Then ask some more questions.

➤ Have your agent be present to interpret and advise in case an issue arises.

➤ The inspection should not be a top-secret, subversive plot to kill the deal. It is an informative experience. Allow the homeowner to be present. There may be a logical explanation for a puzzling circumstance.

➤ Don't let a cracked plinth block kill the deal.

If You're the Buyer's Agent

As the agent for the buyer, you are usually responsible for arranging the inspection. You have experience in this field and are familiar with the various inspectors and their modus operandi. Contrary to popular belief, most of the repairs inspectors deem necessary are inexpensive, so don't let your buyer scare easily. That said, if there is a flaw to be found, you will want the inspector to find it. You don't want to hear that the entire HVAC system blew the day after the closing and that your buyer had to pay for it, because he will always hold you responsible. Similarly, your counterpart, the seller's agent, will also hope that the inspector finds any flaws before the closing. If a deficiency is found, the seller can correct the problem before it erupts into a lawsuit, complete with attorney's fees and damages. It is always better for both sides if any legitimate shortcomings are uncovered by an inspector prior to a sale.

Hints to Buyer's Agent

➤ Get a thorough inspector. Offer several to the buyers, or refer them to the Yellow Pages.

➤ Explain the comments of the inspector to the buyers while on the site. Settlement cracks seem to expand in the minds of the buyers after they leave.

➤ Explain which items are the responsibility of the seller and which are the responsibility of the buyer. Ask the inspector to estimate the cost of any repairs that the buyer will have to make (even if you already know).

➤ Before the closing, you should have a walkthrough with the inspector to ensure that the repairs were made to his satisfaction—not to yours, the buyer's, or the seller's. The inspector detected the flaws and suggested specific repairs; now he needs to determine whether the repairs are adequate and in line with his recommendations.

If You're the Seller

Sellers usually worry themselves sick over the inspection—at times, rightfully so. Many states are now requiring sellers to disclose any known defects in their homes. These laws will greatly increase the income of attorneys in those states, because proving a person knew about a defect can be difficult. Many times, things break that the seller simply didn't know were defective. That's the reason for the inspection. In fact, obvious problem situations should be addressed before the home goes on the market.

Hints to Seller

➤ Don't try to hide the shortcomings of your home. A plant over a carpet stain or a cloth over a cracked commode top will cause the inspector to reach for his fine-toothed comb.

➤ If you are asked to leave the premises during the inspection, make available any warranties, as well as receipts for any repairs that you have had done while in your home.

➤ Don't worry. If it ain't broke, you don't have to fix it.

If You're the Seller's Agent

Get the name of the inspector in advance and seek background information on this person. If you've never encountered him before, try to get the scoop from others who might know: Is he usually fair? Too harsh? Inexperienced? Great at his job? There are vengeful inspectors out there. Dealslayers, in fact. They have pictures of unsold homes on their walls and have mounted shingles with the addresses of their kills engraved on copper tubing. Make every effort to attend the inspection in order to defend the home and support your client.

The seller's agent should be thoroughly familiar with the house and able to answer questions posed by the inspector. In the event that Inspector Clouseau has decided that the sellers should not partake, the seller's agent should arrange to have the sellers available by phone so that they can provide any needed information. (In my experience, it is better if the sellers are not present as they may speak sellerese and disclose a bit too much information.)

Hints to Seller's Agent

➤ Do a Superman imitation: fight for truth, justice, and the American way.

➤ If it's broke, somebody's gotta fix it. Working tactfully with the other agent and both sets of clients, decide who will fix it, and when, at the inspection.

➤ If you smell a dealslayer early in the inspection, call for reinforcements. Ask an inspector or a builder who you know and trust to look at the perceived problems.

— REALTY CHECK —
Raving Over Inspection Report
(with Apologies to Edgar Allan Poe)

Once upon a midnight dreary,
While I pondered weak and weary
Over a torn and tattered
  inspection-of-a-home report;
While I nodded, nearly napping,
Suddenly there came a rapping
As of someone gently tapping,
  tapping at my chamber door.
"'Tis a Realtor, nothing more."
She bore a paper to my door.

Then I looked at all the writing,
All of it concise and citing
Broken these and leaking thats
From the ceiling to the floor.
I knew that if I called the buyer
He'd think the seller was a liar
O'er the home's inefficiencies
Contained in the inspector's lore.

I'd known the house was somewhat lacking,
But did not expect the whacking
That the agent came a-packing
And delivered to my door.

It all began so soft and sweetly
As the buyers had found the house so neatly,
And made an offer so discreetly,
Expecting to move in with no chores.

The sellers prepared a full disclosure
Of the structure's current composure
But had listed and reported all was kosher.
Then when the inspector went to peeking,
He noted that the sink was leaking, leaking
a lakelike puddle. A puddle on the kitchen floor.

Not to appear befuddled,
In an attempt to be subtle,
He placed a towel upon the puddle
to absorb the water and muddle
That adorned the kitchen floor.
'Tis a sink leak, nothing more.

With a whirl the man inspecting
Grabbed the thermostat, selecting
Temperatures from an age forgotten,
A clime from the season enjoyed before.
He sniffed the air, soon detecting
something burning; unsuspecting,
We all thought we'd smelled it before
'Tis some dust on the heat exchanger, nothing more.

Although he was somewhat aloof,
He examined the asphalt roof.
He began to mingle with the single shingles
As his body began to tingle
For he had not ascended
To such a height before.
There is some wear here, nothing more.

He then descended,
His knees bended and his clothes about him rended,
For his wife had never mended
Stockings or breeches before.
It was in the hot September,
This inspection, I remember,
And the buyer, vain of temper
Would require all repairs, as he'd said before.

The seller stated, unremorseful,
That the buyer had been most resourceful
In providing a course full
Of the house's lore.
He would repair the kitchen sink,
The HVAC going on the blink,
And threw in the roof with a wink,
As he left to meet his shrink.
Quoth the inspector, nevermore.

Chapter 11

The Mortgage

Little House on the Variable

When Charles Ingalls built his little house in Walnut Grove, he didn't have to worry about a mortgage. As he accumulated money, he bought materials and added on. Now, the Japanese have 100-year mortgages, and American homebuyers can shop at a mortgage company as if choosing cantaloupes. You can thump and thump until one feels right.

For example, you can thump ARMs, which are adjustable-rate mortgages. An ARM can adjust annually, or every three years, or at the end of five years—or even at the end of seven. Some adjust twice a year. In any case, the borrower is at the mercy of the market and the anniversary date of his particular ARM. Timing is everything.

In 1990, rates were fairly stable all year, until Saddam Hussein invaded Kuwait. That day, the rates shot up so fast that a Patriot missile could not have intercepted them. Rates stayed high for several days until President Bush sent the troops over and the nation became sortie friendly and realized this was nothing to lose interest over. Rates returned to normal.

However, the borrowers whose loan anniversaries happened to fall during those four days when rates soared o'er the ramparts had to live with those rates for another year. Four days out of three hundred and sixty-five the rates were high. It probably cost thousands of borrowers millions of dollars.

Usually, big houses have higher price tags than smaller ones. If you purchase a larger, more expensive home with a variable-rate mortgage, remember that when those interest rates go up by two percentage points, you'll feel it more than your neighbor in the smaller, less expensive house. For instance, if you have a $60,000 loan you'll pay an additional $60 payment; but if you have a $200,000 loan, your payments will increase by $200. For that reason, if you are going to have a house on a variable rate, make it a little house on a variable.

If You're the Buyer

Be aware that although the institutions that share their money with you, the borrower, are called lenders, they can be divided into four subgroups: benders, menders, penders, and renders.

Benders comply with all federal regulations, but give the borrower the benefit of the doubt. Fannie Mae has more guidelines than the Constitution. The courts interpret the Constitution in all sorts of ways—some liberal, some conservative. Benders feel that FNMA (Fannie Mae) can be interpreted in different ways, too, and they are correct.

Benders are usually found in the person of the mortgage loan officer, who is sometimes referred to as an originator, for he originates the loan. (Some originators should be called terminators.) Individuality plays a large role here. The lending world is no different from the rest of the world. Some loan officers are slackers, and others are diligent brain-rackers who will work with you.

Menders are originators who can repair bad credit. Not everyone who has bad credit deserves a bad rap. Fannie Mae is a forgiving woman; she can be convinced that the borrower is contrite and should be absolved of any past sins. Mending involves more work, which is why many people in the lending ranks turn their backs to people with bad credit.

The penders are usually folks who want to be benders but lack the smarts, or who try to mend but lack the gumption. They collect all the necessary documentation, quote good rates, but somehow cannot manage to close the loan. The interest rate can only be locked for sixty days, but the deal is not yet approved. They always need one more thing. Sometimes penders will take three months and still not get an approval.

Last, we meet the renders. They take one look at the sales price, the credit report, and the borrowers and then begin to gnash their teeth, beat their chests, pour dirt on their heads, and rend their clothes. The only loans they want are no-brainers—for example, the borrowers have $5 million in the bank, have worked for the same employer for ten years, and want to borrow $30,000.

Hints to Buyer

➤ Let your agent guide you through the borrowing process. Rates and discount points aren't everything. You may be quoted half a point lower by a pender and end up paying a higher interest rate with a bender six months later.

➤ Ask the lender for a recent reference. As with the Realtor, the inspector, and the rest of the motley crew you're mixing with, you will ultimately pay for his services. So get references.

➤ Have your information ready—all loans, account numbers, addresses, places of residence, landlords, mortgage companies, places of employment, their addresses, tax returns, pay stubs, etc.

➤ Truth-in-lending statements are lies.

➤ Good-faith estimates are not.

If You're the Buyer's Agent

If you've been doing this for a while, you probably have a "pet" loan originator or loan officer you've worked with successfully in the past. As an agent-and-lender team, you have joined forces to pull through borrowers whom renders rended or penders pended. You have fought Ms. Fannie Mae while bending like a tree in a hurricane or mending like a seamstress in a hurry. You should make it your job to know which financing program will work for this deal. Should the seller pay some points? Should the buyer go conventional or FHA? The mortgage loan safari is a trip through thick forest that intimidates, humiliates, and often infuriates the borrower. Stand by your client.

Hints to Buyer's Agent

➤ Make the buyers aware of every avenue of financing available. Let them know why you feel they should go the way you propose.

➤ Warn the buyers about penders and renders.

➤ Describe the loan application in great detail. Have the buyers prepared.

➤ Attend the loan application with them. Loan people often make statements that scare buyers to death.

➤ Warn the buyers that a "truth in lending" statement is not ever the truth and that a "good-faith estimate" is really a hedge against a lawsuit if the lender really blows it.

If You're the Seller

You are so relieved to have found a buyer for your house. You have survived the War of the Worlds and all that preceded it. But, as Yogi Berra once said, "It ain't over till it's over." The method of purchase may have ramifications for you, the seller.

If the home is being purchased with a loan guaranteed by the FHA, then your property must meet certain structural and cosmetic criteria. Unless stated otherwise, the seller is responsible for the costs incurred completing these repairs. Loans guaranteed by the Veterans Administration require the seller to pay all discount points. Likewise, Fannie Mae may require you to have your dwelling conform to local building codes.

Hints to Seller

➤ Have your agent explain, as soon as possible, your responsibilities associated with the loan that the buyer is attempting to obtain.

➤ If the buyer is assuming your loan, have the lender explain the potential of your liability. You don't want to end up with two little houses on the variable.

➤ After the credit report and deposit verifications are in the lender's hands, a determination can be made as to the likelihood of the loan being granted. If everything is in order, relax.

If You're the Seller's Agent

You will learn from the buyer's agent exactly to whom the buyer will apply for a loan. At the appropriate time, you will communicate with the lender to see if there should be any concern. The lender cannot divulge specifics of the loan and will not breach the boundaries of confidentiality. But, if all is well in Lendingland, that information may be passed on.

As the seller's agent, you may want to meet the appraiser to ensure that the appraiser is aware of the comparable sales on which you and your client based the sales price. From time to time, a selling agent can help an appraiser understand the value of a home. Appraisers are always open for sales information because that allows them to provide the best service.

Hints to Seller's Agent

➤   Communicate with the buyer's agent.

➤   Communicate with the lender.

➤   Meet the appraiser at the home. Be prepared to share your data and assist in the appraisal.

➤   Keep your sellers informed. Prepare them for the road ahead.

— REALTY CHECK —
Knowing the Score When You Apply for a Mortgage

Ironically, not long ago, foreclosures on residential real estate reached an all-time high in the United States, right around the time that the economy was in recovery and interest rates had fallen to a forty-year low. This all made for some serious head scratching and finger pointing within the financial sector, which had made all the "bad" loans. Why were so many folks defaulting during these otherwise healthy economic times?

A look into the credit scoring practices used by lenders across the nation offers a solution to this puzzle. These financial institutions have defaulted to FICO credit scoring as a means to qualify loan applicants. The Fair Isaac Corporation developed the FICO score in the 1950s and the Federal Trade Commission has approved its use.

Credit history is monitored by three different companies: Equifax, TransUnion, and Experian. The FICO score is determined using these agencies on the basis of their reports. A great FICO score is 800, but anything over 720 will allow a borrower to be approved. Any score under 600 will force the borrower to pay a higher interest rate.

For years, determining how credit was scored was a mystery, but new information has emerged explaining the fundamentals behind FICO. (For you college football fans, this formula makes as much sense as that used in the Bowl Championship Series.) The score is weighted as follows: 35 percent, payment history, with more weight on current history; 30 percent, capacity, which is the amount of credit available to this borrower; 15 percent, length of credit; 10 percent, accumulation of debt in the last twelve to eighteen months; 10 percent, mix of credit.

That explanation is as clear as the air in L.A.

Additionally, I would assume that the "Fair" in "Fair, Isaac" is a personal name, not an adjective.

In FICOland, paying off debt and closing the account is not a good thing. As financial experts are quick to point out, consumers should realize that eliminating credit lines does not help improve their credit scores, since 30 percent of a person's credit score is based on capacity or available credit.

For years, the syndicated talk-show host Dave Ramsey has told his listeners that they'll be at peace once they eliminate their credit card debt (he refers to the demolition of credit cards as "plastic surgery" and is a huge proponent of the operation). This is good advice, so it seems odd that the opening of credit accounts is viewed as healthy while retiring debt and closing accounts are scored negatively. Here's an example of what can happen if you try to be a conscientious consumer: When one woman realized that she had a credit card that she no longer used and didn't need, she canceled it. And then her FICO score plunged 30 points. For reducing her ability to accumulate debt, she was punished. If she had been in the process of buying a home, her chances of being approved for a loan would have been reduced.

One reason credit cards are so profitable is that the lenders who offer them know that people will spend more money than they have, therefore paying interest on the debt, not to mention late fees and finance charges, which are highly lucrative for the lender. Credit card companies and retail outlets have brainwashed consumers into thinking that it is acceptable to spend money that they do not have.

"Gold" and "platinum" cards hold even more allure. If a person has a certain card, then affluence, success, and invitations to all the right parties follow—don't they? No, all that follows is a larger bill at the end of the month.

It seems that a person with less access to debt would be a better risk for a home mortgage than a person with opportunity to charge the seventy-two-inch plasma television and the living room suite immediately after a home purchase. Accordingly, it would seem a closed account is better than an open one. But that is not so.

Chapter 12

The Closing

It Ain't Over Till It's Over

By the time the closing rolls around—and it does—all four combatants (buyer and buyer's agent; seller and seller's agent) are fit to be tied. The sellers have told their agent that they hope their house caves in on the buyer and the buyer's agent immediately following the closing.

The buyers can't believe the sellers have denied them unlimited access to their future home over the past several days. They were "packing to move"—what a flimsy excuse to disallow admittance. The agents have made every attempt to shield their clients from the shrapnel flying from inspectorial explosions and financial institutional blasts. Both sides fear a dogfight as the buyers and sellers meet to close the deal.

The agents warn their clients. "The water is under the bridge," "Don't burn any bridges," and other bridge analogies are offered as the agents hope themselves to be bridges over troubled waters. The buyers and their agent and the sellers and their agent arrive. Papers are shuffled, pens are produced, the closing is under way. Suddenly, as soon as the last "i" is dotted, the last check is handed over, and the final piece of paperwork is signed in quadruplicate, a strange metamorphosis occurs and the buyers and sellers become Eddie Haskells.

"Hello, Mr. Seller. Isn't it a lovely day?" the buyer offers. "I hope we will be able to maintain the wonderful quality of life that you have so tremendously manifested during your residency."

"Oh, you're too kind. We just hope we have left the home in a condition worthy of your inhabitance," the seller Haskells right back. "By the way, we left that refrigerator for you . . . kind of a house-warming gift."

"Sheesh!" both agents groan, with rolling eyes.

If You're the Buyer

The closing is the closing. Once closed, it cannot be reopened. The documentation is written in legalese and will be paraphrased by the closing attorney or an agent of the closing attorney. Most of the forms meet governmental guidelines, and the language contained within the body of the documentation cannot be changed or amended, even if the buyer does not agree with it. The numbers, however, are supplied by the lender. The lender, be it a bender, mender, or render, can make a mistake. Many have, many times.

Hints to Buyer

➤ If you feel you should read every word of every document you sign, get copies the day before the closing. Ask questions then, not at closing. The closing agent may not have the knowledge to answer all questions.

➤ Compare the figures disclosed to you in the truth-in-lending statement to those on the closing statement. If they differ, either way, ask the question. Even if the error seems to be in your favor, the head-in-the-sand tactic won't make it go away. It could haunt you later.

➤ The attorney and your agent are being paid for their work. If you have a question, ask now, or forever hold your piece (of property).

➤ If your parents are so inclined, this is a great time to let Ma and Pa meddle, but only if they are offering to pay off your mortgage. I heard a good story recently. One Pa, a high-ranking corporate executive who never signed anything without having his attorney vet every piece of paper, came to a closing and was concerned with the vast numbers of documents his daughter was to sign. He quickly called his attorney and asked if he could fax all the documents to him for review. The attorney asked the father the price of the house. "It's $500,000," the father reported, finger poised on the fax machine's Send button. "Does your daughter have $500,000 cash?" "No." "Do you want to give her the $500,000 cash now?" "No!" "Then have your daughter sign the papers and don't bother me anymore." The attorney wasn't just being brusque (okay, rude); he was being logical. The only way you are going to gain possession of a $500,000 house (or any other property at any price) is if you sign the papers at the closing, or produce the cash.

If You're the Buyer's Agent

You will coordinate the closing with the buyer, the seller's agent, the lender, and the closing attorney. You will assist the buyer in obtaining documents that are conditions of the closing. These conditions could include termite letters, "notice of completion" forms, inspection releases, and other paperwork.

Despite the thoroughness and preparation by all parties, problems can still surface prior to the closing. For example, a problem could arise if, at a reinspection, a defect is noticed that was missed at the first inspection. Or termites could suddenly appear. Or maybe a loan question comes up. Just remember: These (maybe literal) bugs can be fixed.

Hints to Buyer's Agent

➤ Get a copy of the closing statement and pertinent financial data before the actual closing. Check everything, from the address to the tax proration.

➤ Follow up in a couple of weeks to ensure the recorded deed and title insurance policy have arrived. (Normally, the title insurance commitment is given at closing.)

➤ Try to go over the statement before the closing. Tensions are running at a fever pitch during most closings.

➤ Know your stuff.

If You're the Seller

This is the magical moment that you have long awaited—the reward for the valor you exhibited in the face of the enemy. Now is not the time for a surprise, but here are some common (surmountable) ones I've encountered:

➤ The survey may show that a driveway encroaches upon an adjoining property.

➤ A mechanic's lien may have been filed by the plumbingly inept but legally expert plumber, whom the seller would not pay because the plumber did not complete the work to the seller's satisfaction.

➤ The mortgage balance was higher than expected, or there may have been a shortage in the escrow account.

Yikes! But don't assume you'll have to toss this deal out the window and go back to square one. Usually, hitches like this can be worked out, especially if both parties are prepared, patient, and persevering.

Hints to Seller

➤ Get the closing information as early as possible in order to clear up any problems. There could be a delinquent taxpayer with your name who has caused Fannie Mae's uncle, Uncle Sam, to place a huge lien on your little home.

➤ If you have a HUD (Department of Housing and Urban Development) loan, closing the first day of the month as opposed to the last day of the previous month will cost you one entire month's interest. On a conventional loan, the same situation would cost you one day's interest. Interesting.

➤ Communicate with the institution that holds the loan secured by your property. Talk to your agent.

If You're the Seller's Agent

At the execution of the sales contract, you should have informed the sellers of the approximate amount of money they would net from the sale of their home. Between then and the closing, unexpected expenses could have arisen, such as termite extermination, repairs required by the lender, or removal of a lien or other encumbrance. As these problems arise and are resolved, you should rework the figures to let the seller know the new amount they can expect to net from the sale. Be prepared with a final figure at the time of the closing.

As the seller's agent, you will work with the buyer's agent, the lender, and the closing attorney to schedule repairs, final inspection (walk-throughs), and, finally, the closing. Then you and the buyer's agent will don the appropriate Ward or June Cleaver face and head to the closing to meet the two sets of Haskells.

Hints to Seller's Agent

➤   All the work you have done in the past will be quickly forgotten if you have made an error or failed to notify the seller of an expense that appears on the closing statement.

➤   Get any "surprising" information from the closing attorney in advance, examine it, and be prepared to react quickly, if necessary.

— REALTY CHECK —
Closing In on Insurance—Before You Close

The president of the National Association of Realtors noted that the next big challenge facing our industry is . . . homeowner's insurance. Huh? Not radon, mold, war, terrorists? Nope. Homeowner's insurance or hazard insurance.

According to a State Farm executive I contacted, State Farm is no longer offering homeowner's insurance to new customers in seventeen states. A person who is not already a customer of State Farm would be unable to buy from State Farm in those seventeen states.

If homeowner's insurance vanishes, will lenders continue to make loans on real estate? Never! The sky is falling.

One insurance agent believed that the insurance

industry, like most industries, is cyclical. He stated that the industry has been very competitive over the past twelve years and that premiums have risen since 1990. "But the insurance companies have begun to lose money on homeowner's insurance," he notes. "The loss ratios on homeowner's insurance are horrible."

The underwriting guidelines have been tightened significantly. In the past, a person could contact an insurance agent hours before closing on a house, and a binder insuring the place for hundreds of thousands of dollars would magically appear at the closing. All this, for only a few hundred dollars.

The insurance companies now run an Insurance Bureau Score on the buyer and the property in order to determine whether the buyer is creditworthy and the dwelling is insurable.

If the dwelling has had a "water loss," a claim based on water damage, most insurance companies will not write a policy, because water encourages the growth of mold.

Most mold specialists ("industrial hygienists" is the term they prefer) will admit that there are approximately 20,000 types of mold of which about four are toxic. But that is enough to produce an avalanche of lawsuits against insurance companies. Though mold is excluded from almost all insurance policies, one broker told me that its exclusion has not slowed the lawsuits.

Yet another agent pointed out that homeowner's insurance was created for catastrophic losses, such as those caused by tornadoes or fire; but, he believes, it somehow evolved into a maintenance policy. He has had claims for paint spilled on carpet, for kitchen counters scorched by hot skillets. He noted the stringency of the Insurance Bureau guidelines: in one case, a buyer had qualified for a $500,000 bank loan, yet his insurance credit report was such that he was denied insurance.

One buyer was told the house he wanted was uninsurable because the prior owner had made two claims based on plumbing leaks. Only when the company was informed that those leaks came from a hot tub that had since been removed was coverage given.

Premiums will continue to climb. Houses and homeowners will be categorized as preferred, standard, and substandard by insurers, and premiums will be priced accordingly.

The next new contingency in real estate contracts may be "This contract is contingent on Buyer's ability to obtain homeowner's insurance." Don't start your hunt for a good policy at the eleventh hour; do be patient, despite the frustrations that come with the territory, and be prepared to read the ever-changing fine print.

There's another twist. In addition to a regular

homeowner's insurance policy, title insurance is an essential consideration for new homeowners. Until the early to mid-1980s, when a home was purchased, the lender received a title insurance policy. This policy assured the lender that there were no liens or encumbrances on the property; it made no exception for boundary disputes, and there was no requirement for a survey.

Title insurance is expensive. For example, on a $300,000 home, a policy would cost $1,600. If the owner also wanted a policy, that was an additional $1,600. To charge $1,600 for two policies for which only one set of research was needed and that insured against the same matters seemed expensive.

The title companies agreed and lowered the fee for the buyer to about $35. This was well received by buyers, who were receiving the benefit of a $1,600 policy for a fraction of the cost.

But it turns out the two policies are not the same. According to Elizabeth Smith, an attorney with the Nashville law firm Mudter, Morgan and Patterson, "The owner's policy will contain an exception for disputes in boundaries, whereas lenders will not accept a policy that contains an exception for survey matters." As a result, if there is a boundary question, the lender can require the owner to remedy it; however, neither the lender nor the title insurance company has any liability or responsibility. Ms.

Smith noted that unless there is a "true, staked survey," the buyer is, in fact, at risk of boundary disputes.

To further complicate matters, lenders no longer
require a mortgage loan inspection. The mortgage loan
inspection was often misunderstood to be a survey of
the property. In fact, it was a plot plan citing boundaries, easements, encroachments, the house, the driveway, and any fences or walls that existed. In closings,
the closing attorney would explain to the buyer that
the mortgage loan inspection was *not* a survey and that
a staked survey should be performed before the construction of fences, walls, or home additions.

It was not unusual to see highlighted areas indicating that a fence currently was on the wrong side of
a property line or that a corner of the house was outside the building envelope. These encroachments
were dismissed as standard fare, and the buyer went
into ownership oblivious to the complications that
could ensue.

In one case, a property owner had his lot sur-
veyed with the intention of building a fence. Upon
his return home from work that evening, he noticed
a stake in the middle of his neighbor's backyard.

"You know what that is?" the neighbor asked
rhetorically, then answered: "Your property line." The
owner's lot had grown by 25 percent while the neighbor's lot was reduced by about the same percentage.

In virtually all real estate transactions, the buyer demands a home inspection in order to ensure that all components of the house are functioning properly. Since the land is valued at 25 percent to 33 percent of the purchase price, it seems that it, too, should be inspected prior to purchase.

If you're told that "your" fence is two feet over your property line, but that your neighbor doesn't mind, that does not ensure that the next neighbor will feel the same. If the house next door is sold, the new neighbor can require the owner to remove the fence. The same applies to a driveway, a patio, deck, or even a part of the main dwelling.

Title insurance will not cover this type of situation, nor will the lender accept responsibility. The homeowner-to-be should have a staked survey of the property done to ensure that the purchase includes the land beneath the improvements—improvements being the home and all that goes with it.

Chapter 13

Foreclosures

Fool's Gold

Non-real-estate people have considered foreclosures the best deal in real estate since the day the Indians traded Manhattan for a few beads. This misconception has been perpetuated by some unscrupulous people who have written books and conducted seminars telling people how much money anyone with a pulse can make in the purchase and resale of foreclosures. (And I thought buyers and sellers were liars!)

How do you think a foreclosure happens? Maybe the lender hides in the bushes and waits until the precise moment when the homeowner has the place in its most perfect condition; then, before the unsuspecting borrower can say "due process," the lender foreclosures. The whole process must take about ten minutes.

The best is yet to come. The lending institution then sells the property for approximately a tenth of what it costs to foreclose, because of an obscure tax law that is unknown to anyone except peddlers of get-rich-quick books and a friend of a friend of a friend who knows someone who bought a foreclosure for $3,000 and sold it for $1 million. For some reason, despite his real estate prowess, this someone still works at the same job he has had for the last twelve years and drives a '77 LeSabre with a rotten dashboard.

If You're the Buyer

Buyers are misinformed about the value of foreclosures. Lending institutions are regulated in pricing the properties they sell; the price is based in part on the appraised value of the property. In foreclosures, the lender is usually barred from accepting any offer lower than appraised value for the first several months.

These foreclosed properties are referred to as OREO ("other real estate owned") or REO ("real estate owned"). Each lending institution has a department that deals with REOs. The heads of these departments are frequently at the whipping post in officers' meetings. The reason for this is that the officers who initially lent the monies for the purchase of the REO properties can't believe that the REO department head can't receive offers better than those that actually came forth.

Many times, in an effort to move these undesirable properties, the lender will offer better than market rates for financing. This could be a red flag. In condominium purchases, this may cause problems, especially if the new owner should need to sell the property. In order to receive a Fannie Mae loan, the developments must be 60 percent owner occupied. Even lenders that don't participate in Fannie Mae programs view developments that are more than 50 percent investor owned unfavorably. If the development is not approved by Fannie Mae or her cousin Freddie Mac, the new purchaser will not be able to obtain financing. In short, as the buyer of the REO you may have gotten a great price with unbelievable terms. However, the property may not be sellable.

Hints to Buyer

➤ If you're searching for the deal of a lifetime, read the next chapter. The chapter you're now reading is about foreclosures, and they are not the deal of a lifetime.

➤ If you must buy a foreclosure, apply the same

caution and discretion that you would to a non-foreclosure.

➤ There's a reason that the previous owner allowed the foreclosure: the property wouldn't sell.

If You're the Buyer's Agent

The buyers have heard of a friend of a friend of a friend who made a million on a foreclosure. Because they smell money, buyers don't view foreclosed properties as they do non-REO properties. They are excited, and the little things don't matter. They don't want their bubble burst. Visions of gold at the end of their rainbows often cause the buyers to beat a path to the nearest bank and sign anything placed before them.

Hints to Buyer's Agent
➤ Treat the REO just as you would any other property.
➤ Provide a CMA and explain the value of the property.
➤ Deal with the lender as you would any other seller.
➤ Understand the pressure on the lender's representatives who must deal with you. They are accustomed to receiving offers that would make

other sellers slit their wrists. And if you think a spouse or Ma or Pa can be tough, try a table full of bankers.

If You're the Seller

The sellers in this chapter are corporations, so you probably don't fall into that category. But read on for more insight into this aspect of foreclosures, in case you ever find yourself trying to sell one.

The corporation that is selling has spent a rather tidy sum of money on the foreclosure, and now it is a property owner by default. Literally. The previous owner probably tried every way in the world to keep the property out of foreclosure—that is, to sell it—but could not. Now the lender must try to sell it. It orders an appraisal. It must list the property for the appraised amount or its own basis (which includes acquisition and foreclosure fees), whichever is greater.

The property is almost always empty and often poorly maintained. There are reasons the lender owns it. Nevertheless, a naive public views the property as a deal, which often elicits stupid offers.

Hints to Seller

➤ Reject stupid offers. Let the buyer know you are a lender, not a giver.

➤ List the property with a licensed real estate agent. She will ally herself with you as you face the sharks.

If You're the Seller's Agent

Even though the seller is usually a well-funded, well-staffed lending corporation, it will frequently retain the services of an outside selling agent, rather than handle the matter in-house. If you're appointed the agent, you must deal with (or duck) calls from every variety of quack out there. These callers have seen the television ads, spent a fortune on a book filled with misinformation (lies, if you will), and now they are official, card-carrying entrepreneurs. They need to be reprogrammed and debugged of the hype they have ingested so that you don't waste hours with this version of the next Donald Trump.

Hints to Seller's Agent
➤ Alert the buyers to the fact that your responsibility to the lender-seller, even though it is a corporation and not an individual, is the same as your responsibility to any seller.
➤ Don't advertise the property as a foreclosure.
➤ Tell the fools not to count their gold.

— REALTY CHECK —
When a Flip Is a Flop

From time to time, most real estate agents receive the "flip" telephone call. "Hey, I've stumbled into a little money and I think I'd like to invest it in real estate. If you ever see something I could buy and flip and make some money on, let me know. My brother and I could even throw a little paint on the walls if we had to."

It has often been remarked that every generation thinks it invented sex. The same is true of flipping houses. In most cases, the only thing flipped is the buyer's net worth, often in the wrong direction. That's not to say that real estate can't be a profitable, stable investment, particularly under the right market conditions. In my hometown of Nashville, there have been periods when property values escalated at a rate of 3 percent to even 10 percent per year.

When prospective buyers are searching for housing in hot markets and the search extends into a second year, they are shocked to find that a house similar to one they could have purchased twelve months ago for $110,000 is now $130,000. In many cases, the trauma is so severe that they never buy.

However, determining the exact moment that the appreciation will occur is impossible. Anyone who has dabbled in the stock market has a fish story—the tale of a stock that would have made them millions if they had only held it a bit longer or sold it a bit earlier. The same is true in real estate.

If a person has $20,000 or $30,000 and wants to invest in a rental property in a rapidly appreciating area, that is usually a sound idea. The rent will cover the debt service and the property can be depreciated while it appreciates.

But the flipper, that's a whole 'nuther animal. Just as many question whether that ol' celebrity Flipper was a dolphin or a porpoise, while some think both of those are fish, so confusion attends the notion of flipping houses versus the idea of investing in real estate. There is a whale of a difference.

Very, very rarely will a house enter the market priced at a small percentage of its value. When it does, the listing agent learns of his miscalculation in a hurry. The home will be shown more often than a Paris Hilton video and will get more offers than Ms. Hilton did after her performance.

If a house is offered for sale at a ridiculously low price, it is wise to offer more than the listed price, with no contingencies as to financing or repairs, and a closing date at the seller's discretion. If you want to play this game, you have to move very quickly. I always chuckle when I hear about the flipper wannabe who is contacted with news of a $250,000 house hit-

ting the market for $175,000 and who responds he
will have time to look at it toward the end of the following week. If he is able to view the property the
first day, he decides that he needs some time to think
it over and, my favorite, "run some numbers." Numbers running is for bookmakers, not for investors, especially flippers.

Chapter 14

The Deal of a Lifetime

Yes, Virginia, There Is a Santa Claus (and His Name Is Spelled A-G-E-N-T)

One morning a man called me and told me that he had heard I could get him "the deal of a lifetime." I informed him that I had been fortunate enough to work with people who had fared rather well in their real estate investments. We then spoke about his situation, resources, goals, and other pertinent data. He was very open with me and several times told me that he did not want "just a good deal" or even "a great deal." He wanted "the deal of a lifetime."

I assured him I would keep an ear to the ground and use all my resources in an attempt to get him his deal. Furthermore, I promised that I would not call him until I had found the absolute deal of a lifetime.

That afternoon, the man called again. He informed me that he had left his home for about thirty minutes and had forgotten to turn on his answering machine, so he had probably missed my call.

"What call?" I asked.

"Well, it's been three hours," he explained. "Haven't you found it yet?"

"Found what?"

"The deal of a lifetime!" he screamed.

I had failed him.

When people decide they want the deal of a lifetime, they mean the deal of the lifetime of a housefly (about seven days).

If You're the Buyer

There is a Santa Claus. He has elves. In real estate circles, elves are disguised as real estate agents, lenders, and closing attorneys. The reindeer are the MLS and the network of agents. The deal of a lifetime will raise its head on occasion and may appear as an agent's mistake, a seller's mistake, a corporate buyout, an estate sale, a home lacking street appeal, a secret . . . or once in many lifetimes of deal-finding, a foreclosure.

Christmas can come at any time. If you haven't been a good boy or girl (karma again), you will not receive the gift. Be good and have your jolly elf (agent) on the lookout for the DOL (deal of a life-time). On occasion, an agent from an area that does not demand a high dollar per square foot will venture into uncharted waters without the help of a map (CMA). Or maybe an ogre, in an effort to greedle without an agent, will price his house too low.

Multiple-heir estate sales are often profitable. For example, if there are five heirs and if the buyers and sellers are $1,000 apart in price, that represents only $200 per heir. These negotiations can become very intense, what with the inevitable emotional bag-gage. If one heir gets too tense, step outside for some fresh heir.

Some companies will arrange for the purchase of an employee's home if they transfer the employee. A relocation specialty firm will usually handle the sale for the corporation. They purchase the property at a discount price and attempt to profit from the sale. If the relocation company obtained an unusually low appraisal and negotiated a low buyout, a DOL is in the works.

Hints to Buyer
➤ Get to know Santa Claus (an agent) and his elves.
➤ When the real-estatic Christmas comes, regard-less of the month, put out your cookies and milk (earnest money).
➤ Be nice.

If You're the Buyer's Agent

You have been warned not to come back to your buyer unless you return with the deal of a lifetime. It's time to work fast with the buyer in arranging the financing, the inspection, and the closing prior to finding the property that is soon to become the deal.

Deals do not stay on the market long. If a possible DOL property comes on the market, you must act quickly and efficiently. The inspector should attend the first showing; there may not be time for a second before the deal is snatched out from under you and your client. The smart buyer's agent realizes the offer must be clean because it will probably be presented with several others. A clean contract for a lower price is worth more than a higher, contingency-loaded offer.

Hints to Buyer's Agent
➤ Work with the elves. Have the reindeer harnessed and hitched to the sleigh.
➤ Convince the buyer to submit a cash, no-inspection, quick-closing offer. (This applies only to the deal of a lifetime.)
➤ Communicate. Some lesser agent will sell them a lesser deal.

If You're the Seller

Did you sell for too little? Depending on your personal circumstances, perhaps it actually made sense to do so. Then again, perhaps it didn't.

Hint to Seller

➤ No one made you sign the contract. You have no one to blame but yourself. If you haven't signed yet and you have a hunch that your pain is someone else's gain (DOL), stop and reevaluate the situation before you put pen to paper.

If You're the Seller's Agent

You should understand your client's needs. Perhaps a quick, low sale will allow her to realize a profit in another area.

Hints to Seller's Agent

➤ Familiarize yourself with your client's motives. Does she need to sell at this price? Does she need to move so quickly?

➤ Don't blow it, if this is what your client wants and needs.

➤ Don't worry. Everybody loves Santa Claus.

— REALTY CHECK —
The Top 10 Lies in Real Estate

Think you know everything now? Then get out there and buy (or sell—we can always use the inventory) . . . but here's a final reminder to watch out for the Top 10 whoppers.

10. The truth-in-lending statement is true. The truth-in-lending statement discloses APR (annual percentage rate), which can include fees such as discount points, origination fees, and prepaid interest. The APR *never* reflects the actual interest rate of the loan, and therefore the truth-in-lending statement never does, either.

9.   Buyers and sellers can expect counteroffers. Many a deal comes undone when a seller thinks that the buyer expects a counteroffer. If you receive an acceptable offer . . . accept it!

8.   A clear termite letter guarantees no termites. Termite inspectors can only inspect what they see, and they can't see inside walls. Always assume that a house has termites and treat the house as soon as you buy it. The cost of treatment will spare you the much larger cost of treating damage if it occurs.

7.   You don't need your own real estate agent. "I can represent both sides," says the listing agent. Walk away from this person. No agent can effectively handle both sides of the deal. Every party needs his or her own representation.

6.   The basement never leaks except in a hard rain. If the basement shows signs of leaking, it's going to keep leaking, no matter the weather, until you get it fixed.

5.   The appraisal establishes the actual, definitive value of the house. The market, and the market alone, determines the value of the house. So, when the market speaks, the appraiser should listen. If a house is under contract for $100,000 and the appraiser says it is not worth a penny over $95,000, get a second appraisal.

4.   The buyer's loan is approved. Even if a buyer can produce a letter from a lending organization saying that her loan has been approved, she still can derail the loan by making choices that damage her credit rating right up to the closing. A seller shouldn't consider a buyer's loan approved until a check is in their hand at closing.

3.   Advertising sells houses. Advertising exposes your house in various media, but no one has ever bought a house just from reading an ad.

2. *All houses are priced 10 percent over the price the seller is willing to accept, and there is always a cushion.* Most houses are priced on the basis of recent comparable sales. Overpricing a house can harm its chances of selling at a good price; therefore, most houses are listed for their true market value.

1. *The biggest lie in real estate—"I can't afford that house."* Nine times out of ten, the buyer *can* afford it. All that's needed: a good Realtor who can guide him professionally and honestly through the process.

Afterword

Living Happily Ever After

Now you're ready. You can prevail. Whether you're the buyer, the seller, or an agent, whether this is your first house or your fifteenth, it's time to assemble your team and press on.

Laugh in the face of ogres. Stand strong in proud defense against the Greedles. Open your heart, soul, and closet to Woodward and Bernstein.

You now know how to achieve your goal. Ally thyself with thy agent (or thy client) and prepare for the excitement. Brew some tea in the kettle as Ma and Pa meddle. Place a ladder against the wall for the inspector. Leave your love light on for the ETs. Prepare for a Closing Encounter and make sure you have enough ink in your pen to sign all those pieces of paper.

Acknowledgments

This would not have been possible without the help of my friends Donald Seitz; his wife, Maureen; and his son William.

Thanks to Tommy Patterson for forcing me to attend the seminar that gave birth to this book.

The Simon & Schuster consortium of Nancy Hancock, Sarah Peach, and Martha Schwartz, along with hired gun Becky Cabaza, accomplished miraculous deeds.

And, as always, my wife, Beth, was by my side willing this to happen.

Thanks, everyone.

Index

personal memorabilia, 21,
22–23
pest control companies, 77–78
pets/animals, 13–14, 22, 24
points, 118, 121
possession date, 98–99
prequalifying, 59
price
asking, 87
and buyers, 92–93
and characteristics and functions of real estate agents,
6–7
contract, 94
cushion, 158
and deals of a lifetime, 154
determination of, 11–12,
36, 61–62
and flipping houses, 148
and foreclosures, 142
high, 6–7, 14, 16–17, 19,
48, 61, 92–93, 158
and listings, 11–12, 14,
16–17, 36, 158
low, 87–88, 148
and non-agent listings, 36
and offers, 79
and open houses, 48
parents' reactions to, 70
Realtors' knowledge about,
4
reduction in, 14, 61–62,
83
and sale, 92–94, 97
and seller's agent, 63
seller's original, 53, 80
and top ten lies, 158
See also offers

priorities
of buyers, 81–82
for repairs/renovations, 27

Ramsey, Dave, 124
real estate agents
blaming of, 13, 17
crazy things said and done
by, 6–9
and deals of a lifetime,
151–58
and foreclosures, 146
impressions of, 37
and listings, 11–12
needing own, 157
paradoxical dilemma of, 92
and parents, 70, 72
Realtors differentiated from,
2
reputation of, 97
See also buyer's agent; seller's
agent
Realtors
characteristics and functions
of, 1–9
commissions for, 3, 4, 5, 35,
36, 40, 63
differences among, 4
finding/selecting, 4, 5
and first-time buyers/sellers,
5
handing-off of, 5
knowledge of, 3
and non-agent listings, 35,
36
real estate agents differentiated from, 2
references for, 118

recording of deeds, 19, 131
references, 118–19
referrals, 59
relocation, employee, 153
renders, 117, 118, 120
rental properties, 148
REO (real estate owned), 142–43, 144
repairs/renovations
  and closings, 133
  cost of, 108
  and flipping houses, 148
  and inspections, 108
  and listings, 14
  and mortgages, 120
  prioritizing of, 27
  and street appeal, 30
  See also improvements

sale
  and buyers, 92–94, 97
  and buyer's agent, 93, 94–95, 96
  and contingencies, 94
  and contracts, 94
  and negotiations, 93–94
  and offers, 94–95, 96, 98
  and price, 92–94, 97
  as sacrifice, 91–92, 95
  and sellers, 96–97
  and seller's agent, 93, 97–98
sellers
  buyers' relationship with, 61–63
  and closings, 127–28, 131–33, 134
  and commissions, 40, 43
  corporations as, 145–46
  and deals of a lifetime, 152, 155
  debt of, 53
  disclosure of defects by, 108–9
  first-time, 5
  and foreclosures, 145–46
  and inspections, 107, 108–9
  lenders as, 141–47
  and listings, 11–15, 20
  and mortgages, 120–21, 122, 157
  most prevalent mistake of, 88–89
  motives for selling of, 52, 155
  and moving, 99–100
  and non-agent listings, 35–44
  and offers, 12, 79, 81, 83–85, 86–87, 88–89, 156
  and open houses, 46–48
  original price paid by, 53, 80
  and parents, 74
  quirks of, 26
  relationship between seller's agent and, 49, 97–98, 122, 134
  and sale, 96–97
  showing of houses by, 15
  and street appeal, 26–27
  and top ten lies, 156
  See also owners
seller's agent
  buyer's agent relationship with, 19, 75, 110, 121, 122

About the Author

RICHARD COURTNEY is an award-winning real estate broker and a celebrated author who writes a weekly real estate column for the Nashville *City Paper*.

Buyers Are Liars & Sellers Are Too! provides information gained from Courtney's sale of more than 850 properties since 1978. A member of the board of directors of the National Association of Realtors (NAR), he has served as the federal political coordinator for U.S. Representative Jim Cooper and is the Realtor's Political Involvement Committee (RPIC) representative for Tennessee.

Courtney has been voted "Realtor of the Year" by the Greater Nashville Association of Realtors (GNAR) and "Best Realtor" by readers of the

Nashville Scene. He has also received the GNAR "Lifetime Award of Excellence" and the "President's Award" for his work in affordable housing. Courtney will serve as GNAR president in 2007.

Courtney is a certified real estate brokerage manager (CRB), certified residential specialist (CRA), and accredited buyer representative (ABR). He has also served on the board of the Tennessee Association of Realtors.

Courtney is an alumnus of the University of the South in Sewanee, Tennessee, and resides in Nashville, Tennessee.